PANDORA'S
GARDEN

John Griswold, series editor

PANDORA'S GARDEN

Kudzu, Cockroaches,
and Other Misfits
of Ecology

CLINTON CROCKETT PETERS

The University of Georgia Press
ATHENS

© 2018 by the University of Georgia Press
Athens, Georgia 30602
www.ugapress.org
All rights reserved
Designed by Kaelin Chappell Broaddus
Set in 10.25/13.5 Quadraat Regular by
Kaelin Chappell Broaddus
Printed and bound by Thomson-Shore, Inc.
The paper in this book meets the guidelines
for permanence and durability of the
Committee on Production Guidelines
for Book Longevity of the Council
on Library Resources.

Most University of Georgia Press titles
are available from popular e-book vendors.

Printed in the United States of America
18 19 20 21 22 P 5 4 3 2 1

Library of Congress Cataloging-in-Publication Data
Names: Peters, Clinton Crockett, author.
Title: Pandora's garden : kudzu, cockroaches, and other misfits of ecology /
Clinton Crockett Peters.
Description: Athens : The University of Georgia Press, [2018] | Series: Crux, the
Georgia series in literary nonfiction | Includes bibliographical references.
Identifiers: LCCN 2017058470| ISBN 9780820353203 (pbk. : alk. paper) |
ISBN 9780820353210 (ebook)
Subjects: LCSH: Introduced organisms. | Introduced organisms—Control. |
Weeds. | Weeds—Control. | Endemic animals. | Endemic plants. |
Human-animal relationships. | Human-plant relationships.
Classification: LCC QH353 .P4745 2018 | DDC 578.6/2—DC23
LC record available at https://lccn.loc.gov/2017058470

for Yumi-chan

Contents

Prologue
SEAGULLED

Age six, donning a white jogging cap of my father's and wandering the beach of North Padre Island, Texas, I felt the seagull dung land on my head with a spectacular splatter. I didn't know what it was. I had assumed all birds were winged automata, cartoons that hovered in the air, never eating nor bodily functioning.

There was nary a cloud in the ocean-sprayed sky, so I presumed the good Lord had dropped a hailstone of an ice cream scoop as a reward. The cream poured across the cap in a trickle. God must have thought I'd been good, entitled to his little gift on a hot shoreside day. So I slid a finger across the dung and inserted it in my mouth.

The first question was, why was it so warm? And salty. The crunching sensation was surprising, the cream containing grits or sand, the pasty substance gumming my teeth. Then a fire spread through my mouth.

I sprinted to the ocean and, knee deep, cupped seawater over my lips. The brine at first muted but then multiplied the scorching on my gums. I screamed and bolted for my aunt's condo, my mouth sandy and raw.

I like to say, sometimes, that this is why I've become an atheist.

Though this is just a punch line, I have become agnostic about one thing: human knowledge of our place among other creatures, knowledge about the living things layered around us that serve as bricks in the architecture of our lives.

———

For about a year, my family of Texans lived at the ocean's edge in a condo we couldn't afford, rented to us by my millionaire aunt. The walls were papered with colonialist-imagined Hawai'ian scenes: bikinied women in grass skirts, white men with shotguns, pigs roasting on spits. The door of my room opened out onto the Gulf, the water off North Padre not beautiful but a slate gray as if a storm were perpetually approaching. Oil derricks smoldered offshore, and container vessels plied between shoals. Half the time, the sands were filled with jellyfish.

I don't have fond memories of the beach, but the dugout of my memory leaves me with two things that live on vibrantly besides God's ice cream: the distant horizon of water, and the tumultuous tornadoes of seagulls that soared over our shores.

That the expanse of ocean is a metaphor for unknowability is almost as obvious as how people who lived in our condo thought about seagulls. They believed them nuisances, slaughter-worthy. Pests, flying roaches, mice with wings.

One day not long after my seagull encounter, I was granny-shooting Cheetos into the sky to urge the circling birds to dive-bomb. While a gull swooped down, an orange-tanned, middle-aged manscape approached my mother and demanded that I stop feeding the pestilence. Spittle flew from his mouth. He shook his fist. My mother and I were speechless. He scowled and walked off, not before swiping a hairy orange paw at the sky as if he could murder the creatures out of the air.

"Seagull" is a misnomer, a term used by many Americans for any bird found near the ocean that's not a pelican. There are at least twenty-eight gull species in North America, dozens more shorebirds. This detail and list of birds has been reduced to an amorphous mass of shadow that hovers over tanning legs and nips french fries from oyster shacks. They are winged terrors, a plague phenomenon, and nothing more.

A ten-minute drive south from my aunt's condo lay the Padre Island National Seashore, where half of the birds in North America can be seen at various times of year, including many gulls. The 380 birds that check into the Padre Island National Seashore don't all rest comfortably. They land because luck and eons of evolution bid them to. They eat salty foods found under thin layers of foot-turned sand. Some turn aggressive because the meekness of humans selects for that, an evolutionary response to our civilization. They operate on chance and the chemicals that roll around and fire and spark and wish to keep them alive. Which isn't so far from myself at age six.

I try to picture an average decision made on an average day by a six-year-old. What to eat, how to feel about friends, neighbors, whether to escalate an argument. Language overlays instinct: fight, flight, rest, digest, empathize, and resist. Many decisions employ logic, that hallmark of human development, but many do not.

I was a boy who was raised religious, and so I was. I wore a cap because my mother told me to, but I wandered the beach outside adult supervision because my energy furnace burned so hot. The beach was there. So were birds. I liked the taste of ice cream.

I'm thinking, in a half-squinty long view, what was so unseagull-like about me? Wandering a beach, happy to have a burst of dessert from a divine creature created, many believe, to explain natural phenomena we once couldn't fathom, when in reality my untoward gift was secreted by a bird whose bodily functions I didn't comprehend.

What was human about this transaction, this meeting of species, was maybe that I thought the term "ice cream." But I'm no longer very interested in what separates humans from animals and birds, especially those we don't like and tend to kill a lot of. I think Western civilization has spent the last three thousand years codifying what makes us philosophical and seagulls seagulls. We've also been making other humans into nonhumans, and I'm interested in that too.

I'm curious about Western civilization's connections to bugs, rodents, snakes, and aggressive seabirds, not because I want to good-witch-transform them, but because I think there are some surprising similarities between how we've acted toward other humans and how we've acted toward those we chose to perceive, discuss, and categorize. Especially those life-forms who slither, hide, proliferate, soar above, and drop their mysteries onto our heads.

PANDORA'S
GARDEN

The Miracle Vine

At the 1876 Centennial Exposition in Philadelphia, Alexander Graham Bell revealed his telephone to the world public. The Sholes and Glidden company displayed the first Remington typewriter. Heinz launched its ketchup. And Charles Elmer Hines introduced the first commercial root beer. There were more than two hundred structures housing 30,000 exhibitions, including elephant-sized cannons, a 1,400-horsepower steam engine, and the right arm of the Statue of Liberty.

But according to the journal *American History*, the exhibit that drew the most "ooohs" from the cosmopolitan crowd of ten million was a garden display of a fast-growing Japanese vine. With leaves the width and shape of a human palm, the evergreen produced conical clusters of spring flowers that were the color of plums and smelled like red wine.

Later at the World's Columbian Exposition in Chicago in 1893, Charles and Lillie Pleas of Chipley, Florida, saw the same presentation of the vine and learned it could grow almost anywhere. It was drought tolerant, heat tolerant, frost tolerant; it could thrive on the barest of soil. It was a legume, like a pea, so it fixed nitrogen into the earth instead of siphoning it out. It had the nutrition of alfalfa and the stamina of timothy grass. What better place to grow it, they thought, than in the eroded, beaten, spat-upon hillsides of North Florida? They could feed it to livestock while it revitalized their earth.

The Pleases planted the vine on their land in Chipley, and the legume thrived, slinking up their front porch and curling around their bench. Because of its success, they sold seeds by mail order catalogue, and their claims of the vine's swiftness and long-suffering robustness led to an investigation for fraud. The Postal Service authorities drove to Chipley and, at the Pleases' property, ran their eyes over a thirty-five-acre field of viridescent hands waving in the breeze. The farm had once swept away, but now livestock were nuzzling the dense vine carpet. The claims about the vines were honest, the Postal Service decided, and they dropped the charges.

As of today, kudzu has spread to thirty-two states and Canada.

It is called the foot-a-night vine, the cuss-you vine, the vine that ate the South. It has leapfrogged the Rockies and taken up home in Washington and Oregon.

Time magazine recently called kudzu's introduction one of the hundred worst ideas of the twentieth century, along with Prohibition, telemarketing, DDT, and the Jerry Springer Show.

The U.S. Department of Agriculture announced a few years ago that kudzu control would no longer be "economically feasible." This from the government that built the Panama Canal and landed twelve men on the moon.

Kudzu's taproot can weigh four hundred pounds. It is self-seeding, and so a shoot of kudzu grows and grows and plants another and another.

People in the South report parking cars and not being able to find them, later uncovering the vehicles from garages of vines. According to historian Kristen Hinman, kudzu has covered railroad trestles so thickly that freight trains have derailed. The walking leaves wrap around utility poles and bring down power lines, snuffing out the light.

Kudzu roams empty lots in Florida, props up mailboxes, swims in unused pools. Sometimes a lawn will be a well-mown postage stamp while next door the yard is shoulder deep in cuss-you. Kudzu blankets cars and trees indiscriminately. It wraps so tightly that it mummifies, killing plants, not by constriction, but by shutting out the sun.

When an unmolested vine crests over a copse of trees and envelops it, the shape it makes is uncannily like the prehistoric creatures that once roamed the Florida swamp. These are called "kudzu monsters," and they can be found all over the South, peering into windows, severing connections, and disappearing into shadow.

Channing Cope of Georgia was kudzu's champion. A heavy-set man, alcoholic, fan of suspenders, Cope was a self-proclaimed front porch farmer. He was in the merchant marine, then a press agent, a lawyer, and then in 1927 he bought a run-down seven hundred acres and named it the Yellow Farm. The land was so ravaged that the county agent, who surveyed it with Cope, said that he would "perish to death" trying to make a living—a statement made no less intuitive by redundancy.

Cope believed farming and life could be easy. With a telescope and electronic switches to open cattle pens, a "farmer could run his land from an easy chair." Kudzu's uninhibited growth made Cope's front-porch corralling possible.

Cope discussed his farm on his weekly radio show. On air, he was sometimes drunk, a people's person, speaking clearly if flamboyantly—a Howard Stern of the Depression. He was the editor of the *Atlanta Constitution*, which had a circulation of two hundred thousand. In his daily column, "Channing Cope's Almanac," he wrote about the ills of things such as barbershop quartets, his dead dog Mr. Burns, erosion, and, ironically, alcoholism.

He became known as the Kudzu King or the Kudzu Kid, as *Time* magazine called him in a 1949 profile. In the same story *Time* called him "fat" and reported that he spiked his morning coffee. Cope started the Kudzu Club of America. The organization had twenty thousand members by 1943. They met annually and had contests to see who could plant the most vines.

Each year they elected a bright and beautiful Kudzu Queen.

———

Florida cherishes its trees. In Tallahassee you can witness the roads divided around oaks that locals refused to uproot, named like pets. Canopied streets and thin highways should be four or six or eight lanes, but that would necessitate chain-sawing many cypress and pines and magnolias that drape their agile arms over the snaky roads, dripping their moss the way a mother covers a child in the wisps of her nightgown.

"We're all tree huggers in Florida," an old, jewel-bedecked woman will say on a plane bound for Tallahassee, looking out the window to see Florida's beloved ocean of green.

Soil erosion was more than just an economic problem for Cope. It was a "national menace," he wrote. "It's children's shoes and clothes and school books, it's the labor of the past and the hopes of the future . . . Soil erosion is not merely topsoil being moved off the land. It is school erosion, church erosion, and family erosion."

Cope taught others to plant legumes to combat this "demon." Kudzu was, he said, "the miracle vine."

He hosted officials from many branches of the government and foreign officials from as far away as China. He encouraged and provided for the planting of kudzu by poor farmers, as did, soon, the U.S. government. The Civilian Conservation Corps and the Soil Conservation Service planted some 100 million vines on road banks and public lands. From 1935 to 1945, kudzu acres in America jumped from ten thousand to five hundred thousand.

Cope's best means of dissemination was his weekly radio broadcast from the creaky floors and big swing bench on the Yellow Farm porch. Cope eloquently, humorously, and volubly championed kudzu, every week on Wednesday at 4:30 p.m. His editorials in Atlanta's premier newspaper also helped kudzu's cause, and they were reprinted in *Business Week*, *Reader's Digest*, and *Gentleman Farmer*. He became Georgia's "Conservation Man of the Year" in 1945. That same year he and his wife answered three thousand fan letters.

Cope knew kudzu was pernicious. He received mail every month from people also asking him how to get rid of it. Some of his listeners and readers didn't like the vine crawling on their porches, snaking up telephone poles, peering in their windows. They accosted Cope on the street.

One detractor was James Dickey. In his poem "Kudzu," Dickey wrote:

> In Georgia, the legend says
> That you must close your windows
> At night to keep it out of the house.
> The glass is tinged with green, even so.

But this was not the time for weak stomachs. The ground was disappearing. "Our position," Cope wrote, "is in some respects like that of the physician who discovers that his patient is suffering from a malignant fever, say malaria. He does not prescribe warm baths and massage and manicures and hairdos and soft music. He produces his arsenic and quinine and atabrine and his frightening hypodermic needle and goes to work."

A sign standing outside Chipley's Ag Center today reads:

KUDZU DEVELOPED HERE

Kudzu, brought to this country from Asia as an ornamental, was developed near here in the early part of the Twentieth Century and given to the world as a soil-saving, high-protein forage plant by Mr. and Mrs. C. E. Pleas. The fast-growing, deep-rooted leguminous vine has been widely grown in the United States as a drought-resisting erosion-controlling plant that compares with alfalfa in pasture and hay-making values.

Florida Board of Parks and Historic Memorials

The sign hangs under the Florida state flag, shadowed by an elm and dwarfed by the Washington County Agriculture Center sign. It is the kind of marker you'd pass by and not read, or read half of and shrug.

Behind the sign and the Ag Center is a forest of live oaks, and in their leaves and limbs drip the Suzy-Q curls of Spanish moss.

Spanish moss is neither Spanish nor moss. It's a pineapple native to Florida, its tendrils used by Native Americans as long as three thousand years ago for pottery and flame arrows. It was used by European arrivals for upholstery. If left unchecked, Spanish moss can kill trees. It will blind them, like kudzu, encasing leaves, sealing off the sunlight, the curtains pulled down on a southern scene. But imagining the South without Spanish moss cascading from trees would be like imagining the West without cactus. Spanish moss is a scene setter, the marking of a part of country and culture.

The same might now be said of kudzu. It seems to have taken on a distinct southern appeal, gothic because it swims well with the idea of something taking over.

Besides preventing erosion, Kudzu has a variety of uses. It can be dried and woven into baskets, coasters, and a host of other household flotsam. Some people knit kudzu into hats. Others make skin cut sealers. Some southerners erect kudzu Christmas trees. Cows love it. Sheep will munch on it, as will goats.

You can make soap with kudzu, and certain medicines. Scientists at Harvard think they may have stumbled on a drug made from the vines that could cure alcoholism. The sickness for drink may be abated by a taste for kudzu. You can buy supplements made from ground miracle vine, vitamin bottles advertising "liver support," "anti alcoholism," and "liver tonic."

It is also edible. The plant is nutritious, after all: it is 9 percent protein. The Japanese dry it, grind it, and use it as a pudding. People in Japan cannot believe that the vine that grows innocuously throughout their country and is used in desserts so closely associated with childhood would have taken America by the throat and begun to shut out the light.

One reading of *Frankenstein* is not that our nature-defying creations run amok but that, once created, once brought into this world, they are not embraced. We turn away, so our creations become monsters.

Inside Chipley, near trailer parks, in the Piggly Wiggly, at the tree nurseries, at the Ag Center, people know about the miracle vine.

Especially for a giant patch, they say, right around the corner, the three-story kudzu monster behind the Piggly Wiggly. It resembles a mansion draped for fumigation. Subtropical-marine leaves, each with four little nubs, a creature with ten thousand hands. The vines have spread across oaks, cypress, and the electric wires flanking trailer houses. The leaves fan across the street. They are outstretched, praying to sky.

The vine is crowding out natives, shading the life out of them, but perhaps there is righteousness in the science fiction arc. This monster—created, brought over, set loose, unloved—it seems proper that it should be running around and killing the things Floridians cherish.

Cope hung on to the idea of his miracle vine, even when he began hearing reports of "out of control" vines and when the government stopped recommending its planting. When Channing Cope became older, a constant drinker, and kudzu was delisted from the USDA's recommended conservation plants, he refused to clear out the tangles that were then spreading from his land. It covered neighbors' trees and crowded the road. In 1976 the people who bought Yellow Farm found that kudzu had "devoured" the seven hundred acres as well as Cope's house. The vine had enveloped its owner and all of his life.

On a muggy summer morning, the Colonial Restaurant in downtown Chipley advertised a "Southern Style buffet" for $6.99. Fried corn bread, mashed taters with cream gravy, fried chicken, collard greens, and sweet iced tea.

Corn is from Central America, and potatoes are from Peru. Chickens and black tea hail from China. The cream in the gravy is a product of cattle from the Fertile Crescent, in present-day Iraq. The Colonial Restaurant's table sugar is sucrose refined from sugarcane, a process discovered in India. Collard greens are probably Brazilian.

These exotics have invaded the local vegetation by becoming agricultural products, and eaters at the Colonial Restaurant soak up this southern sense of normalcy, the whitewashed walls, two bear-skins and an alligator's head hanging from the ceiling, the Lion's Club, or whatever it was, European descendants meeting at a long table.

They sipped and chewed and swallowed, perhaps unknowing that at that moment something unstoppable was lurking in the collective places where they forgot to check, the basement, the window sill, atop the very oaks that shaded the Colonial Restaurant. Both foreign and native, both unnatural and cultural. The monster, which was us, how we've made the world, unleashed at night, was there, ready to envelop them.

The miracle vine crept, night by night, foot by foot, over Cope's driveway, until one day the way out was shielded from sight. With so much kudzu cover, teenagers took it as an opportune time to drive into Cope's fields, party, and make love underneath the leaves.

Kudzu shuts out the sun. Why not our headlights and heated embrace? The moon in your eyes is like a kudzu plant tonight, my sweet—so green.

Cope came one night to run them off. He took three steps, stepping off his front porch, where he'd broadcast for decades, took three steps to chase the hooligans from his Yellow-now-green Farm, to prevent their uncouth behavior among his miracle vines, the alcohol that kudzu could have fought many years later in pill form saturating his blood, thirty years of his life now deemed "undesirable," he who built the ecological monster, took three steps and died of a heart attack and fell among the leaves like hands, waiting to catch.

Rabbits and Convicts

Before gunships, stolen children, and sextants, Australia was the land of sleeping gnomes that used their giant feet to shade themselves in the broiling heat of day. It was the home of dogmen, whales with fangs that snacked on frigates, and lithe, bare-breasted, shimmering mermaids. It was the twin city to Eden, where angels reclined in fields of gold, spice, and sandalwood.

The Roman geographer Pomponius Mela proposed the existence of a southern continent, Terra Australis, in the first century, and Ptolemy later agreed, on the theory that without it, the Earth would topple over into space.

In this way Australia became a balance of heaven and hell, as it is still, though home to a new legion of angels and demons. The plights of the Europeans and rabbits in Australia mirror each other in that they point up the myths that we Westerners are trapped by and tell ourselves as we hop about and wander the Earth.

In 1688 a lost Englishman, William Dampier, grounded on Australia's northwest coast. He was the first to record encountering indigenous Australians. He found them sleeping on the open beach with no clothes and no tools, nor did they have anything to trade. Dampier declared, confidently, redundantly, "The inhabitants of this country are the most miserablest people in the World."

Likely the first European visitors to the sixth continent also included illicit Portuguese, banned by the Treaty of Tordesillas. This pact had divided the newly discovered parts of the Earth longitudinally between Spain and her neighbor, an invisible hemispheric fence cutting the world in two.

But then came Captain James Cook, the Englishman who, at a time when most people were imprisoned by circumstance in their hamlets, would travel across the world three times, land on all seven continents, and solve the scurvy mystery before sailing to the warm seas of Hawai'i, where he would try to kidnap a native king, get stabbed to death on shore, and himself, the captain, be cooked.

Cook's duty on his first transglobal voyage was tracing the arc of Venus across the sun at 40 degrees south latitude, near Tahiti. This, it was thought, would reveal the Earth's position in the solar system and the galaxy, our place in the order of creation outside our horizons.

After the measurements were taken (incorrectly, it turned out), Cook was assigned to discover Terra Australis, which he in fact didn't believe existed. He sailed to the South Pacific and around New Zealand before giving up. He steered for home, west instead of east, and on April 19, 1770, he struck Terra Australis on the nose.

Australian history would be a familiar story to ecologists who study invasive emergence. When an introduced species (sometimes itself endangered) is brought to a habitat where it hasn't lived before, it can, without warning, force other species to the edge of existence. Australians have done this with countless flora and fauna. House cats now carpet the country and tear apart families of songbirds. Cane toads were imported to protect sugar plantations from insects but, instead, have hopped over to wetlands and taken over. One million camels roam and munch in the Outback, along with wild boar, feral goats, water buffalo, and of course rabbits.

In his surrealist children's book The Rabbits, illustrator Shaun Tan portrays Australia's colonization. The arrival image is a crooked, colossal frigate piloted by English rabbits sporting tricorn hats elongated to fit their ears. Their ship's bowsprit bears down on an expanse of Australian beach, while native marsupials cower out of sight. First the rabbits befriend and offer gifts to them. Then the book progresses, through Gonzo-esque images, to show conflict, assimilation, and finally the rabbits rounding up the marsupial children into concentration camps. The last scene is of a single young marsupial befriending a bunny around a pool with the sun setting behind them. The native has managed to escape and is fleeing for its life. The baby rabbit has yet to decide whether to help or to hop away.

Rabbits are popular as pets in Australia and around the world. They have giant, illogical ears, tender, twitching noses, jaggedless cheeks, and lumpy, helpless bodies. For many, they represent not so much a rodent as a baby at the bosom that we want to stroke and let suckle. We care for wide-eyed mammals, goes one theory, as we do our own infants, an evolutionary feature that has allowed us to waste much of our time safeguarding creatures whose survival bears no relation to our own. But our love of rabbits and those like them—foxes, puppies, kittens—can also be seen as our species's saving grace, because it is the instinct that initiates the beginnings of empathy.

Unless, that is, you've been in mortal combat with rabbits, as many Australians have. For Aussies, rabbits are pack killers that swarm. They are locust-style predators, invading a landscape like a tidal wave. If they could, they would eat you.

Though their eyes are color blind, they can see movement over a hundred yards: soaring eagles, fourteen-year-olds with BB guns, coyotes stalking. Their vision is an almost surreal 360 degrees. They can see both sides of themselves at the same time.

In the spring, rabbits, especially males, may carry a white mark on the forehead or a torn ear or a bare spot of fur on the backside, usually from fighting, sometimes to the death. Rabbits, like people, like to sunbathe—hind legs stretched out, white belly up, eyes blinking in the noon light. Until a challenger patters forward.

The ruling-class rabbits enjoy the best food in a warren, the best grazing and territory and mates. The dominants are the last to starve. Lower-ranked rabbits are more likely to poach when a dominant male isn't around. Weak ones are driven from their homes, sometimes for stealing, sometimes just because they are weak.

When Cook went ashore and met indigenous Australians, he strode unapologetically through their homes and thought it curious that they wouldn't touch the ribbons he left on their beds. He found them living in the way William Dampier had described a hundred years earlier. Yet Cook said confidently in his journal that they were stoned happy. "They live," he wrote, "in Tranquility which is not disturbed by the Inequality of Condition." They were, by his reckoning, the leftover innocents from the Garden his people had left behind.

Around the time Hawai'ians were boiling the meat off Cook's bones, Great Britain's parliament met to discuss its poor. Viewed in public periodicals as a sinister mob bent on undermining British morality, they lived in neighborhoods that became known as rookeries, a word reserved in the sciences for dung-smeared nesting sites. Many of them squatted in London's Covent Garden, a once upscale neighborhood harkening to the biblical garden, since given over to refuse and blight.

The poor were called "a swinish multitude" by Edmund Burke and an "excrementitious mass" by Jeremy Bentham. One in eight Britons was suspected of being criminal.

One solution was to kill the problem. Between 1660 and 1819 there were 180 crimes in Britain for which the sole punishment was death. These crimes included picking a pocket, swiping a blanket in the winter cold, and robbing a private rabbit warren.

Half the criminals were allowed a one-time pardon and were branded on the thumb with a hot poker so that, wherever they went, their crime would be known, and they would not be let off a second time.

Great Britain's population tripled from 1740 to 1851. For those petty criminals who could neither cheat death nor flee to America, there were mass graves called Poor's Holes, where they lay shoulder to shoulder, brown hair, blue lips, and yellow cheeks in the open air like autumn leaves in a compost heap.

London was the worst-smelling city in the world, according to the historian Robert Hughes.

"Hell is a city much like London," wrote Percy Shelley.

Rather than continue to kill or mark the new criminals, Parliament looked far east for the disposal of their problem. They decided to offer prisoners seven years in Terra Australis and no return voyage, in exchange for their lives.

Banishment is the oldest punishment. In the Bible, after the apple is bitten, the snake is cast out, then Adam and Eve, and then Cain, to the land of Nod, east of Eden. God marks Cain so that no matter where he goes, everyone will know who he is and how he has sinned.

In 1787, 1,030 people aboard eleven ships, known in Australian lore as the First Fleet, landed on the continent. When the convicts and marines unloaded, all prisoners effectively, there was one gardener on the manifest. No draft animals. No plows, no fertilizer, no proper agricultural tools.

There was a seventy-year-old woman who had stolen twelve pounds of cheese, and an eleven-year-old boy who had stolen ten yards of ribbon and a pair of silk stockings. There were a few highway robbers and prostitutes but not one convicted murderer.

The newcomers beheld an endless stretch of arid monotony: paperbark scrub, gray eucalyptus, loose soil that would not hold a vegetable. They were anchored in an unprotected bay with huge waves that would crash violently on the shallow ground and wreck their tents. They were also met by the natives Cook reported as "happy," who screamed "Warra warra" in their language, which was later translated to mean "Go away."

Like the hundred years' worth of convicts and immigrants that followed, Thomas Austin, a descendant of peasant squatters in West Victoria, wanted rabbits in Australia. Rabbit meat had been a staple of the British diet for the nine hundred years since the animals had been imported from France.

Austin was part of assisted migration committees chartered by Australia and New Zealand with the goal of making the Southern Hemisphere look like England. Sparrows and starlings were shipped in, along with deer, grouse, blackbirds and black swans, insects, trees, and vegetables—all told, hundreds of species.

Austin happened upon the idea of crossbreeding two different types of rabbits, wild-caught English grey rabbits with common hutch-bred domestics that couldn't survive in the wild but were adjusted to the Australian climate.

In 1859 Austin released twenty-four of these mongrels. That same year his neighbor fined a thief ten pounds for bagging a hutch-bred rabbit without permission on his property.

Six years later, twenty thousand rabbits were burrowing on Thomas Austin's estate. In the final decade of the nineteenth century, the rabbits left Austin's land and spread over the country as fast as one hundred kilometers per year.

They carpeted the earth, creating field days for the working poor. Rabbit slaughter factories sprung up, and four million rabbit hides were exported from Victoria in one year. Fifteen hundred tons of rabbit meat were shipped from Australian canneries each year in the 1890s. By that time Austin's neighbor was shelling out twenty thousand pounds per year for rabbit control.

Competition for forage cost the Australian sheep industry half of its animals. The already barren soil eroded. Sixteen species of native mammals became extinct or confined to tiny offshore islands, including four species of wallaby and the short-tailed hopping mouse. Another sixteen became endangered.

Severe drought in the late 1890s, coupled with more and more rabbits and erosion, led to a Royal Commission meeting to talk about the rabbits. This would be the equivalent of the U.S. Congress holding an emergency session to discuss tree squirrels. In 1901 the commission decided the solution to the plague of rabbits was to build the world's longest fence.

They called it the No. 1 Rabbit-Proof Fence, and it took four hundred men working in labor gangs three years to finish it. Two more fences were raised in 1904 and 1906. In total, 8,000 tons of material were used at a cost of $250 per kilometer over 3,000 kilometers across the Outback desert sea.

These were the same fences that Molly Kelly followed for a thousand miles in 1931. Kelly was taken from her mother when she was thirteen along with thousands of indigenous children known as the Stolen Generation, kidnapped from their homes all the way until 1971 in an effort by the government to corral them into Western modernity.

Kelly and her sisters were placed in schools to be trained as servants, maids, or cooks. The three siblings escaped, and since Molly knew that their home lay along one of the rabbit barriers, they followed the fences through the desert for nine weeks. With few provisions, they survived on wild bananas and sweet potatoes. They forded a flooded river, crossed a dried-up salt lake, and hiked through endless-seeming, blinding, searing sand dunes.

And they slept in rabbit burrows.

It only takes two rabbits to cross a fence and continue a plague. The founder of microbiology, Louis Pasteur, aware of the magnitude of the rabbit flood, experimented in laboratories and suggested a disease called chicken cholera to stem the tide. Australians balked at the word "cholera" as they hadn't at "rabbits," and it wasn't until the 1950s that a harmless-to-human virus called myxoma, itself imported from Venezuela, was used.

When the Australian government released myxoma into the country, tumorlike lesions begin appearing on rabbits all across the Outback. The tumors could be so large they would cause the rabbits' heads to swell. Tumored ears drooped to the ground, dragging in the dust.

This was the mark of the unwanted.

Invasive species are thought of as pernicious. But 150 years ago, Australians thought of rabbits as home. Nine hundred years earlier they were French—as, indeed, many English were then, too.

Now, in the dry place where the innocent were stolen, where those already living were invaded, labels like "Eden" peeled off and applied again, where Westerners try to overlay our two-dimensional maps of meaning onto a landscape where texture can't show through, our very notions of heaven and hell and belonging are upended in a generation, as people and plants and animals are trapped by the circumstances of where they are put down.

Yet Westerners still try to draw boundaries, erect fences. We order because chaos is frightening. But where is history not reshaped to fit a fleeting image? We live in the moment, but the things that make up the fabric of our understanding are as transitory as bricks in a toppling wall.

Myxomatosis spread across Australia and infected up to 99 percent of the rabbit population. It was carried by mosquitos, and remains an issue for anyone today who wants to own a pet rabbit in the country. Wild rabbit populations, however, began developing immunities the way bacteria grow immune to medications. Continuing to struggle, the rabbits simply evolved to survive in the arid land where they'd been taken.

To compensate, the government has developed and recommends other modern control methods, including bait poisoning, warren destruction with explosives, fumigation, shooting, trapping, minimal fencing, and biological control with rabbit hemorrhagic disease (RHD). The method favored by private parties, however, is ripping: a tractor or a bulldozer is fitted with multi-tined "rippers," which are dragged over rabbit warrens, shredding and destroying the homes, killing the inhabitants, it is thought, quickly.

Still the rabbits multiply. There are 300 million alive now on the sixth continent. The Western Australia Department of Agriculture's website has guides available for rabbit-extermination techniques, but advises that anyone following them should exercise caution:

"That all rabbits are removed humanely."

Beasts on the Street

I was street-crossing recently when an ancient road hog—the kind
Travolta would approve of—made a swift right turn and roared up
the avenue, its driver lighting a cigarette, unconcerned with, or
oblivious to, the spot where I had been standing two seconds before. My near death put me in mind of the day when I was almost
eaten by the road. I was five years old and in my father's Lincoln
Town Car. This was before air bags and child seats, before people in
Texas cared about seat belts. Riding shotgun, I looked to the right
to see a door lever, fountain-penny shiny, reflecting the soft question mark of my mother's mouth, which she showed me in full as I
opened the door.

I jerked the lever thinking Jolly Ranchers or something would fall
out of the sun visor, some ridiculous notion granted to a child by
James Bond films. I remember the door cracking open onto another
world: a thrash of weeds and tall grass, the song of overhead electric wires, a race of asphalt. The door ajar was an animal's mouth,
tires and road the teeth that would chew me to bits and then swallow me down. I remember the sensation of falling, my readiness
to hit skinning pavement. Fortunately, my mother slammed on the
brakes, and the door squeezed me in an embrace before I could fall
out.

From that moment on, I've been mindful of cars, as I am of any
wild thing. I treat them as unpredictable, mesmerizing man-eaters.
Now, at thirty-five, I hold car culture to be an ostentation of Amer-
icana, an aggressive, cocky, insecure announcement of masculin-

ity. I'm not alone in this, but the piston-whipping phalluses set me on a particular edge because I'm a commuter-biker-walker living in Dallas, a rare thing, like an endangered bird. Here cars prowl the streets, growling in revving ravenousness.

But there's something else: When I watch a no-rate movie like *The Last Stand* (Schwarzenegger's post-gubernatorial "he's still got it" flick) and see a steroided Corvette outpace a helicopter, I feel a mild and unaccountable sense of paranoia. As if the car could burst through the screen and lay me out in my living room. As if I were lost in an urban jungle with metal predators of our own making coming for me.

Before 1900, my ancestors never faced natural selection via car. A century ago pedestrians ruled the roads. Then in 1896 an aging Londoner named Bridget Driscoll stepped off a curb in front of a gas-powered Anglo-French car. The car was cruising at a cool four miles per hour. Driscoll, who was described as "bewildered," concreted in her shoes and the car ran right over her, thus causing the world's first vehicular slaughter. Later, when Henry Ford scattered his Model Ts, with a top speed of forty-five miles per hour, around the globe, the carnage began. Deaths from motor vehicles increased every year of the new century. In the 1920s, 60 percent of those mauled by cars were children under the age of nine.

Lately I've been reading David Quammen's book *Monster of God*, which is about cultures that live near the Gir lion, the Nile crocodile, and the Siberian tiger. These predator-accustomed people put me in mind of my own culture and our acceptance of the death rate by car. In 2013 the number of American pedestrians killed by vehicles—4,735—is forty times the number of people killed by tigers worldwide and two thousand times more than the number of people killed by bears in the United States that same year.

"Their ambivalence toward the [predator] blended nonchalance with contempt," Quammen writes of the people living among animals that sometimes make them prey. The predators represented all of life's uncertainties and were "basically the handiwork of the same spirit, who was devilish or compassionate according to his whim." I think the emblem of American life's ephemerality is the car crash. A fatal collision is an everyday phenomenon, the kind of death, it seems, that is always expected. Death by tiger, by shark, by Florida alligator—these seem sensational only because most of us don't live near flesh-eating monsters anymore and aren't used to imagining ourselves crunched in the vise grip of jaws.

Cars even sound like animals—droning, growling, purring, scraping, rumbling, digesting gasoline. They have "horses" under the hood, "eyes" on their grill, sometimes "fins" and "wings." They are said to "fly," "eat pavement," and "prowl the streets." We even have "monster trucks" and "death cars." They've become beasts, of course, because many of us want them to be. One theory about why we watch so many monster movies is that, removed from the jungle, not having something stalking us in the night feels unnatural. Cars make us feel more like the prey we are.

At the same time, we long to be predators—and want to be monsters. In the latest American Godzilla movie, the monster is the protagonist. King Kong movies show remarkable empathy toward their creatures. And who wouldn't want to be the Incredible Hulk, able to smash apart tanks and bound as high as fighter jets?

We love the part of our kitten that's really a panther. People purchase bears, lions, and crocodiles as if they were shopping for Lamborghinis and Ford F-350s. There are more tigers in my home state of Texas than in the rest of the world. We want very much to be near these beasts, to possess them, because they thrill us with their power. I think they give us hope that we can reach past our skins and become more like the animals we once were.

Wildlife of Unknown Status

Not long ago the largest cat in eastern America, the Florida panther, was categorized by ecologists as "wildlife of unknown status," a label given to ivory-billed woodpeckers, Bigfoot, and the Loch Ness monster.

Until the 1980s the Florida panther was presumed extinct or myth, reported by weary commuters and conspiracy theorists. Tracking one, when scientists realized they existed, required groups of men and dogs reading paw prints, following scent, riding in handmade amphibious jeeps, traversing cottonmouth-filled swamps, and then finally treeing a panther for days. And the cats could jump tree-to-tree.

Even now, how do you study an animal that hunts and wanders in the cobalt of twilight? Panthers swim in the jungle, stalk by stealth. They do not bask in savannas like their African cousins, lazily observed by khaki-clad safarists. They are hunted by searchlight, satellite, and GPS, by nervous scientists knee deep in the Everglades unknown. There are only one hundred to two hundred Florida panthers left in the world, a numerical range that reflects their elusiveness as much as their rarity.

Recently I had the chance to see two very different sides of the Florida panther at the Tallahassee Museum. The Tallahassee Museum is not, as one might think, a concrete and taxidermy repository, but rather a wildlife preserve, zoo theme park, and environmental education center rolled into one, a colorful sensory overload in Florida's capital city.

When I went in July, the museum was almost entirely open air, and the wildlife pens were dirt floors bordered with cypress trees and wooden walkways. Circling the pens were a ropes course for kids and zip lines for the adrenaline-seeking. Teenagers patrolled the grounds with holstered walkie-talkies and Gary-Cooper-in-High-Noon scowls. The museum's animals were almost entirely native: endangered gopher tortoises, alligators, bobcats, red wolves, black bears. Clipart of the Florida panther floated above maps at every turn.

In 1985 the first Florida panther was captured alive by scientists with a drugged deer carcass, confirming its existence. Before that, the most recent Florida panther count had been conducted in 1935 when scientists "collected" eight panthers, fieldwork in those days requiring shotguns.

The day I encountered one, I met a different breed of scientist as well as of wildcat. The panther handler, Mike Jones, and I shook hands on a log bridge, under which swam squabbling otters. His voice vibrated in the same baritone as when, on the phone, he'd agreed to meet with me, a syrupy-southern octave. He was unexpectedly refrigerator-sized, covered in sweat, with a foot-long beard and alligator-bite handshake.

"Now's a busy time of year," Jones said. "But when is it not? We got shipments of sides of beef, cages to clean, otters that are fighting. Schoolkids to lecture. We just put up this ropes course. But it's nice. While the guests scream and climb trees, I get to play with the big cats."

Mike opened a door in a bamboo fence marked "DANGER, RESTRICTED." We huffed across the grassy enclosure and came to another fence made of chain link. A panther curled in a ball on the sand on the other side rose, sniffed, and charged, full-gait, across the grass toward us.

"Here, Buddha, Buddha, Buddha," Mike called.

I'd never faced a panther up close, much less charging. I expected something from National Geographic—a tornado of fur, claws, hissing. But Buddha slowed, and his body slid against the fence, jaw hanging, face molded into a dejected puppy look of pitifulness. The mouth widened and yowled, a high-pitched rusty-door-hinge squeak.

"There's Booty-boo, Booty-boo," Mike said. "Good Buddha."

Florida panthers are, despite popular belief, not purple or blue or black or even dark, but a creamy tan color with an egg-white belly. The most visible difference between them and other mountain lions is that at the end of the Florida cat's fat, ropy tail is a periscope kink, a defect, the mark of decades of copulating with cousins.

Puma concolor coryi once resided throughout the South, its range extending from Virginia to East Texas, an area of 436,000 square miles, more than twice the size of California. That range has been diminished by hunting, trapping, urban sprawl, and poisoning to a paw print of land in Florida, 2 percent of its original home. Florida panthers once commingled with other cougars but have since become isolated in a genetic bottleneck, much like the way the American Kennel Club quarantines its breeds.

In the late 1980s a stereotype developed from the first-caught, not-so-ferocious panther female. The bagged cat was inbred, brittle, anemic, pale-faced, and senile, more like Old World royalty than jungle monarch. After her, the first radio-collared animals kept dying.

The public seized on Florida's rare, sick predator mammals. The media sensationalized the sparse data, and federal and state agencies demanded that scientists carry out more experimentation, field monitoring, and cat bagging. When the Endangered Species Preservation Act was signed, the Florida panther was one of the first species listed.

Probably no more has been done for a single cat: thousands of acres bought and set aside as refuges, inoculation of kittens, steep fines for killing and poaching, construction of corridors so the cats can slink under busy roadways, and protocols to reduce metal poisoning. Injured panthers have even been airlifted by helicopter.

In 1995, Floridians initiated a captive breeding program to alleviate the genetic logjam. Scientists shipped eight Texas female cougars to the swamps of the Big Cypress National Reserve in South

Florida, home to some of the few remaining Florida panthers. After bearing a litter each, the eight Texas females were tracked, tranquilized, and returned to sender.

Buddha, like all Florida panthers, was smaller than most American cougars, but his paws could spread across a basketball. As each paw landed on his side of the fence, it stirred a wave of dust. His ears appeared crinkled but firm, muscular, the arc of his back like a racehorse's, his eyes a penetrating steel blue.

Buddha pressed against the diamond links, and tufts of his fur leaked out. He gaped his jaws, and a canine tooth caught on the steel. Buddha stopped and examined the chain link. When he turned, I noticed his twiggy forelegs, the consequence of a calcium-deficient diet at his previous refuge. Buddha had to make an effort to pick each paw up, otherwise it would drag. He yowled, cried, and even, if my ears were hearing right, purred.

Mike ran a meaty finger through the metal mesh, ruffling the cat's fur. Then he glanced at me, shrugged. "He's spoiled rotten, this one."

Across the pen, a family mingled on the elevated walkway that spanned the panther enclosure. They yelled down, "What's that cat's name?"

Mike peered up, stiffened, but smiled.

"There's two prevailing theories," he said to the family, raising a hand from his wide belt. "One," he counted off, "is to give the animal a name for practical purposes and because it shows we care. The other theory is that a name somehow degrades the cat. That it would make him less animal."

The family nodded their heads and pretended to understand.

"Anyway," Mike went on, "if we named him, people would be calling down all day long, and that might irritate him. We want the guy relaxed."

The family chuckled, nodded, and scuffed on.

"He has a name," Mike whispered, and glanced down at Buddha, whose mouth was still open, mewing. "But we use that just between us."

Later, as I spent an hour gazing down at Buddha from the wooden walkway while family after family passed and yelled down, "Hey, Kitty, Kitty, Kitty," I wondered if perhaps the big cat thought he had another name anyway.

Which would be in keeping with the panther's nomenclatorial history. After the Dutch landed, they reported "lions" in Florida. When the Spanish colonized the area, they gave the cat the Greek name for leopard. Some people still today report seeing leopards in Florida. Others cheetahs, lions, Sasquatch.

There are more than two dozen subspecies of cougar, each closely related to the Florida panther, spread across the Americas. Scientists in just the last decade, after inspecting numerous DNA chains, discovered that any puma female, from Tierra del Fuego to the Arctic Circle, could breed with any puma male. Taxonomically, that made all of the cats, with all these different names, the same.

Florida panther is just one modern variant—one of the twenty-four names for the same creature that presses its jaws against the chain link in front of me, pawing the earth and begging for a cow leg.

Charles Linnaeus was the first to classify the mountain lion as *Felis concolor*, or cat of one color. Inaccurate, because cougars are double-tone—white and tan. The Latin nomenclature later changed to *Puma concolor*. But the name underscores that one of the most widely distributed land mammals in the world, occupying mountains, prairies, deserts, swamps, and forests from Argentina to the Yukon, *Puma concolor* is all one animal.

Buddha the panther, Buddha the puma, catamount, mountain lion, mountain cat, cougar, caterwaul. All these names are for the same animal, and in fact no other species has so many common names for the same thing in one language.

In light of which, Buddha seems like a perfect name: Gautama Buddha, short for Siddhartha Gautama Buddha, otherwise known as P. Sammasambuddha, S. Samyaksambuddha—the Awakened One, the Enlightened One, the Peaceful Enlightened One, or the Supreme Buddha or Sage of the Sakya. The cat in Florida is the same cat in all.

We have not always been so kind to Buddha's incarnations. Massachusetts Puritans in the 1600s once offered five shillings per cougar corpse. In Connecticut you could get twenty shillings for a dead cat. And Jesuit priests in Baja upped the ante to an entire live adult bull for every mountain lion killed.

This was America when predator eradication was not just an economic but a social good, a nature purification. As recently as 1925, Major Edward Goldman of the Bureau of Biological Survey wrote, "Large predator mammals, destructive of livestock and game, no longer have a place in our advancing civilization." Even the Audubon Society was exterminating raptors to spare songbirds.

Predator control roundups in Pennsylvania in the 1700s consisted of men with dogs setting fire to perimeters of thirty or so square miles and driving whatever was inside to the center. On one night in 1760, thirty American colonists torched a miles-wide fire ring, and after a few hours of burning, they advanced toward a golden circle of yelping, growling, clawing predators in a hellish makeshift zoo. In the final ambush, 41 cougars were dispatched along with 17 black bears, 112 foxes, and 109 wolves.

By 1876 Massachusetts, Kentucky, New Jersey, Pennsylvania, Virginia, Indiana, and Rhode Island were emptied of cats. New York, Vermont, and North Carolina soon followed. By the twentieth century, cougars were extirpated from the eastern United States.

Except, that is, for the lone exception, the modern exception: the Florida panther, which, though it was reduced to fewer than fourteen dozen individuals, was able to hide out in the swamp for a hard-lived hundred years.

It's not inconceivable to me that when Floridians see their panther, they see redemption. Something wild was lost from the East Coast, and perhaps it could come back, along with a renewed sense of frontier. The streak of natural purification could be made alive in the glint of a purebred predator's teeth, as if we could erase all the violence that came before it.

———

There were two Florida panthers in the Tallahassee Museum, Buddha and a very wild female, his half sister. The female eyeballed Mike and me from the folds of grass and kept her head down, appraising our fleshy calves, our primate bodies. Later I saw that her pupils were a mix of hazel with a tint of egg yolk, glittery like sharp steel.

"Does she always watch you like you're an injured gazelle?" I asked.

Mike squatted to look across her cage. She was thirty feet away, shoulders tense, lying almost unseen in the bare dirt, grass, and cypress bark. Mike rose up and barked a laugh.

"That still sends shivers up and down my spine," he said. "But yeah, that's just how she is. She was wild since day one. Not mean, just aggressive and really, honestly, more panther."

He directed a thumb toward Buddha. "He's a good cat," Mike said. "You can tell he's more personable than his sister. She has been here eight years, we've fed her every day, tranquilized her for shots, fixed her, doctored her, but when you look into her eyes you just have to know that there's nothing more she'd like to do than make a meal out of you.

"But that's just nature. There's nothing offensive about it. Like I said, she's just the real deal. A real Florida cat. If you like working with predators, you have to get used to the idea that you're helping things that really just want to eat you."

We walked away from the pens and into Mike's office, Buddha still pacing and howling, the female glaring.

Mike cleared a space for me on an old couch against the wall. I was surrounded by icons of predators—canines of all kinds, panthers, lions, sharks, photos and still-life sketches, masks, charcoals, inks, even cross-stitchings. It was a fanged haven.

Mike had worked at the Tallahassee Museum since 1972, but before that he helped relocate the last surviving red wolves back to their home territory on the east coast of North Carolina and to an island off Florida's panhandle. He was currently thinking about the future of the Florida panther, whose habitat, if the Gulf of Mexico inundates South Florida as projections indicate by century's end, will consist almost entirely of the Tallahassee Museum.

"It's a bad deal," he said, and wiped his brow with a towel that had a decal of a panther. "There's no official proposed relocation, no official designated removal site, yet. None that have actively been sought out. We're all so focused on keeping the panthers alive that we're not really thinking about where they're going to go."

I noticed above Mike's paper-blitzed desk a photograph of a Florida panther's body sprawled out on what looked like an operating table. In the photo, Mike had taken the cat's tail and was using it to tickle the ear of a surgeon in a hospital mask.

He chuckled when he saw me gaping. "They're my play toys," he said. "Some people get freaked out by what I do, but I say you can't be too delicate with natural-born killers."

Mike proceeded to inform me of a Florida cat that was tranquilized near Gainesville and misidentified as a migrating Texas cougar—a mistake discovered only when the cat had been driven "home" to Texas. This was not altogether preposterous. A cougar male patrols three hundred square miles. Other than humans, cougars are the most well-traveled land mammal. One radio-collared male, born in South Dakota's Badlands, was tracked migrating east, passing through half of the continent before ending up in Connecticut in 2011, where he was struck and killed by a car. Another puma was tracked swimming across the Panama Canal.

During those perimeter strolls, a cougar male will unsheathe those icepick claws and debark trunks, shovel and sweep together a cairn of dirt, leaves, and twigs, and allot his bowel movements to totems of territoriality. If that doesn't send the message, fighting to the death will.

I wondered aloud to Mike, staring at a pair of mittens with a panther stitched across the knuckles, about how the Florida panther asks the question of belonging.

Does it matter how Florida the Florida panthers are? With normal crossbreeding, they would have been more like other cougars and less inbred long ago.

Mike tensed. "Well, they're Florida cats," he said.

"But they'd be mating with cougars from other places if it wasn't for us."

Mike stroked his beard. "I see what you mean." His fingers caught in the thick rivulets of orange fuzz. I was about to ask another question when he responded further. "But the truth is they're here now. They're Floridian whether they want to be or not. Whether I want them to be or not. I work off the assumption it's best to stop tampering whenever you can."

Then he added after a pause, "Because we can't go back, we just have to continue doing what we're doing."

When I asked about the picture of Buddha in surgery, Mike had explained how Buddha broke his right front leg between two loose planks of a stage at a public show because of his previous diet. Mike and a local veterinarian operated on Buddha and took out a globule of stomach fat and shipped it overnight to a gene clinic in California. Within two days, the clinic grew thirty-four million Buddha cells and shipped eight million to Tallahassee to help patch up the weak tissue. Twenty-six million cells were kept in cold storage.

Thus Buddha now resides on two coasts. If he dies, twenty-six million pieces of him will remain in California, ready to incarnate other flesh.

Mike's morning was busy, and soon it was time to feed the cottonmouth snakes.

The cottonmouth is one of the most poisonous things in North America, or so I read on a placard that adorned its cage, the back of which Mike unlocked. Wanting to continue our conversation, Mike invited me to watch the snake's lunch. Like the panther, the cottonmouth is native to Florida and prefers warm-bloodied meat.

We crowded into a dimly lit room like a janitor's closet, behind the glass displays that faced the museum entrance, with a young safari-clad intern named Suzy. Mike lifted the cage door, and Suzy lured the thigh-thick reptile into a rubber tube with an owl pellet. Using a snake-catcher hook, Mike shoved the reptile into the tube. But the cottonmouth recoiled, the thick muscle rising toward the opening. Mike slapped shut the pen door. The snake snapped at the space where his hand had been.

"You know," Mike said as Suzy glared, "I kind of like it when they do that. I mean, animals lose all the time. Humans have conquered the world. It's so neat to see them stand up to us and be wild."

"This time," Suzy said, holding a tub of water up to the side of the cage, "why don't you hold nature down, and I'll slide this in, so it can clean itself?"

When Mike raised the pen door, he hooked the viper's head with the snake-catcher and wrestled it to the bottom of the cage. Suzy set the tub of water inches away from the squirming lightning bolt and tossed in the owl pellet.

"That's what we get the big bucks for!" Mike laughed and wrapped a beefy paw around Suzy's shoulder. Suzy, of course, went unpaid.

"This is the worst part of my job," she said.

"What's your favorite?" I asked.

Suzy shrugged. "There's really nowhere else in the world to work with a Florida panther. It's really why I came down from New York. I feed the snakes because, you have to take nature"—she turned and slugged Mike in the shoulder—"in all its forms."

Mike and I spent an hour, no less, saying goodbye. We shook hands twice, exchanged phone numbers. Meanwhile, in the sand at our feet, he brushed away leaves and explained to me how sinkholes work.

Water pressure keeps the land floating. But Florida's population is projected to double to thirty-six million by 2060. This is a problem because people will pump out ground water. The ground will collapse around Floridians. Sinkhole insurance claims, for instance, have tripled since 2006.

There is a similar problem for the Florida panther. More people equals more pressure to develop wild spaces into roads, houses, schools, malls, subdivisions. The Florida panther is expected to lose, outside of rising sea levels, another 300,000 acres of habitat to sprawl.

Mike stood up. "We had a sinkhole at the museum a few years ago that was five hundred feet wide. A little after that, one opened up underneath a Porsche dealership a few towns over. Swallowed 'er right up."

He laughed. "There's another victory for nature," he said, and winked.

When Mike and I finally said goodbye, I went to see Buddha again and found him relaxing languidly in an old open-ended barrel that was propped up on its side on crates for him to climb and catch some breeze. His huge paws hung over the barrel's lip like grapefruits dropping.

A family of five frolicked by, snapping pictures. One son, the smallest, went galloping down the planks of the walkway overlooking the panther pen. Buddha stirred in excitement, his eyes darting toward the child. His claws extended and dug ever so slightly into the barrel's wood, the periscope tail twitching.

It was a chilling sight, but the family didn't seem to notice. The mother yelled to her son, "Samson, don't go running like that," but the other kids were busy yelling, "Kitty, Kitty, Kitty," and banging on the handrails that spanned the boardwalk. Their noise was so incessant that I was on the verge of saying something when the father yelled, "Whoa, holy cow!" and jumped a few inches in the air.

There was a hush from the family, followed by gasps as they crowded around a spot in the walkway. They grew quiet until one child screamed and the mother snapped a picture. The father looked skyward and shook his head, rolling his eyes in disgust.

After they left, I walked over to inspect, but I couldn't find whatever it was they'd been animated about. I scanned the palms and dust and ash leaves, shrugged, and glanced at some of the waterproofed panther displays on the walkway. The info boxes were nailed to mesquite trunks and set behind plastic cases. Nailed to a tree nearby was a yellow panther-crossing sign at the border of the panther's pen.

The displays informed me about what the panthers eat (mostly deer and boar), how they play and mate (sex can occur up to forty times a day for three days during ovulation and is violent), and where they live. There was a brown swirl that extended from North Carolina to Texas, where the panthers once ruled. Then there were two blue teardrops in North and South Florida where they are now.

Another display asked, "What is Florida Panther?" And I looked at snoozing Buddha, for the record one-fourth Texas cougar but still carrying the Florida mark in his tail. He also carried the heavy mark of humanity in his upbringing.

And we carried his kin once to Texas, accidentally, and his cells to a freezer in California.

However we chose to answer the question of what he is, the creature that we talked about would still be there and still be rolling over to expose his belly to the sunlight.

Mike's argument for not giving the cat a name is one I'd heard against zoos, refuges, and wildlife rescues: that sometimes, when helping nature, we take the wild out of it. Yet Mike gave Buddha a name, as the Spanish once had, as Floridians do when they help the panther and only "panther," even as they ensure, in the short run, a skimpy supply of genes.

Maybe they wanted it both ways. Maybe it was both ways. Maybe Buddha was in all these things—Florida panther and not.

"Whether chanting Buddha's name will gain me rebirth in the Pure Land or condemn me to hell, I just don't know," wrote Shinran, a Pure Land monk.

There are no pure choices. Frost once wrote: "the best way out is always through," which could work for life or if you're lost in the woods. But in the Florida jungle, the only "way out" is through a serpentine tangle over marsh and alligator nests, around tupelo trees and black bear dens. Beyond the cities and their sinkholes. Through the patrolled game trails and the cairns made from bark, grass, panther shit and piss. The forests swallow up the answers. The cats hide there.

I was about to stroll off when I glanced down between the wooden planks and discovered two yellow eyes peering up from beneath the walkway. The pupils were murky, like two frying eggs, concealed by long grass and wood. The sensation felt like looking down two barrels of a shotgun. A crooked tail twitched.

I wager that Buddha's sister had been locked on to me since I strolled onto the walkway reading about panthers, reading about her. The cat's body hidden, gazing up at the family whose shadows, for a while, concealed hers.

How many hours would she be willing to hide, ready to react to the first movement of mine? Of ours? The wildcat, I realized, had been waiting beneath the yellow crossing sign. Waiting to cross, waiting to pounce, if she could.

The Texas Snow Monkeys

Humans are 99.4 percent chimpanzee. Genetically, we are as close to chimpanzees as horses are to donkeys. Switch a few alleles, cross over a few molecules on the circumambulatory ticker tapes of DNA, and we could donate blood, pour our hearts out into the creatures that swing from trees and thump their chests.

Macaques are only 93 percent chimpanzee, not quite the humanoid doppelgängers. They are naturally shyer than chimps but quickly learn mischievousness. Macaques are the primates you hear about stealing bananas off card tables in Bangkok, puncturing juice canisters for refined nectar in Bali, and, in one bizarre case of ironic justice, knocking from his balcony in India the very politician who was campaigning for their extermination.

Their hijinks and grunts sound vaguely human—which is why NASA used them in the Mercury space project—but if we could imagine them to be people, they would be a very specific breed of *Homo sapiens sapiens*. They are rugged enough to live in almost every climate on four continents, independent enough to walk upright and into the fortified home of their worst enemy, fiendish enough to get what they want when you try to take it away.

Macaques, I believe, are the Texans of the primate world. And this is probably why, though they are not native here, several hundred macaques have been moved, taken up residence, developed a taste for cactus, and become scorned and hated and hunted in the great misunderstood universe of the Lone Star.

Their story begins in central Japan, the land of acacia trees and ver-million maples, the thick buzz of cicadas and the rolling backs of ancient hills like a reflection, one behind the other, into the haze. Tropical storms disgorge salty mists offshore and blow in curtains of rain that leave behind perpetual dew and mud. This is the Japan you won't hear about, the 70 percent of the country blanketed in mountains and forests. The vegetation is so lush that until 1948 a thirty-member macaque troop went undocumented near the out-skirts of Kyoto, a million-member metropolis that happens to be Japan's center for primatology.

But the mountains can get blizzardy in winter, and this is why ni-honzaru are called snow monkeys by the English-speaking world. They are often photographed soaking in hot springs with a bed of powder around the geothermal pools and lining their lips frothily. Some tourists elect to swim in the hot springs, share a bath with a naked primate—an interesting example of what postmodern theorist Donna Haraway in her book *When Species Meet* calls "con-tact zones" of species mingling. "To be one," Haraway writes, "is always to *become with* many." To bathe with animals is to become childlike and an unclothed animal again.

Scientist Eiji Ohta discovered the Kyoto troop in 1948 while look-ing for tree frogs. Hiking off-trail in the foggy summer heat, Ohta was startled by an aggressive, guttural barking emanating from the brush. Knowing there were Asiatic black bear around, he re-coiled and unsheathed a sickle-like knife common among Japa-nese woodsmen. As he backed away, he watched a furry, amor-phous blob jump from the rustling bushes and scamper up a trunk. (Macaques are known in scientific parlance as semiterrestrial, not because they're aquatic but because they spend so much time in trees.)

Ohta moved on, escaping into the undergrowth, his neck and face cascading with sweat. Moments later he looked up while tow-eling off to see a pair of yellow eyes darting from the shade. Ohta re-alized these were the macaques he'd heard about as a child. They'd held mythic status in his hometown, a story the boatmen would tell as they punted downriver. Monkey legends were common, Japan's version of trickster foxes, sly coyotes, and rascally wolves. Primatologist Frans de Waal believes the presence of monkeys in its stories and its forests has given East Asians a better mirror to recognize themselves as animals. He writes in *The Ape and the Sushi Master*, "Seeing primates makes it hard for us to deny that we are part of nature."

Forgetting his fear, Ohta thought he might be able to catch a macaque, drag him and drug him or knock him unconscious with a stick. He took to awkwardly climbing the branches where the macaque sat stilly examining him. After Ohta struggled for thirty minutes, the macaque jumped from his branch to the understory of another tree and from there dropped to the ground and disappeared from sight.

"The figure of that monkey," Ohta wrote later in a scientific paper, "filled me with a mysterious feeling of wonder."

Ohta clued in his colleagues at Kyoto's university, who began leaving out food, drawing the macaques to an open area. After several months the scientists lured the troop to a location for a safari-ranch-like monkey park, a convenient drive from the city and a promising way to pay for their research.

In postwar Japan, after the leveling of the country, many Japanese were looking for something to pride themselves on. The economy, of course, was the most promising arena, and many threw themselves into the labor machine. But *nihonzaru*, "Japan's monkey," indigenous and abundant, became a fixation. More than thirty wildlife monkey parks sprung up around the main island in the 1950s. Each researcher at the Kyoto park took to wearing a large white apron dyed in the center of the chest with a giant red dot, a simulacrum of the Japanese flag.

Gorging on the abundant feed, the troop mushroomed. By 1958 the birth rate had tripled, and the infant survivability rate went from 63 percent to an unprecedented 100 percent. Individual body size bloated. The scientists watched the macaques creep closer, until

they grew accustomed not only to their food but also to their bene-
factors. They morphed from a ghost story told on the river into veg-
etable-stealing tangibility.

Around the mountain and at other parks, macaques began
sneaking into gardens, decapitating cabbages, tearing down
fences, pounding on roofs, scaring children. By the late sixties, national interest waned, and some humans took their revenge. The
Kyoto troop lost three alpha male leaders in succession, all to human hunters.

Then the valley forest was cut down to make paper and room for
postwar sprawl. A power struggle emerged, and the macaque troop
split. The dominant monkeys held the mountain, while the losers
descended into what was left of the valley. With little space to make
their homes, the monkeys rooted in cellars, stole from farms, broke
into and pissed on shrines.

One Kyoto professor, knowing the macaques would soon be exterminated, asked a visiting American colleague on chance, "Would
you be so kind as to accept one of these groups as a gift?"

Lacking indigenous primates, the American thought having a
stable troop within easy observation would be a boon to publish-
able understanding. He and other scientists began meeting to discuss immigration. They wanted their host site to be hilly and for-
ested, as Kyoto is. The new home needed an enclosure to prevent
escape. It needed to be relatively cool, because the "snow" monkeys
cannot sweat. The primates needed to be within easy access of a
major university for study, and to be outside local disturbances such
as mining, agriculture, and drilling. An island off the coast of Georgia would do. Or Hawai'i.

After two years, with a Jurassic Park–like Macaque Island not
forthcoming, the scientists' talk turned practical. They found a
wealthy rancher named Edward Dryden, who offered to house,
feed, fence, and maintain the macaques for no charge at his ranch
in Texas. Dryden's bargain was that he would sell off the "excess"
of the troop on the animal testing market. And so a few macaques
would live confined in cages, try on makeup, swallow pharmaceu-

ticals, or undergo deadening brain surgery while, in turn, a population would be provided for in their new home.

"Revolutionary" confinement, like the prison system of Pelican Bay, California, writes sociologist Zygmunt Bauman, is where inmates are kept isolated from contact. The revolutionary aspect is that there is no need, because of a system of doors and locks and windows, for prisoners to speak, touch, or interact with anyone at all.

"No wonder," Bauman writes, "the victims mount a defense . . . prefer to reject their rejectors."

Twenty years after their arrival at the Dryden ranch, the snow monkeys would move to the Born Free Primate Refuge, a monkey shelter that also rescues simians from test laboratories. Primates raised in confinement for science or domestication grow up biting themselves and sometimes attacking their owners. They go clinically insane. They become dangerous, as one fifty-five-year-old woman in Connecticut found out when a confined pet chimp named Travis, who belonged to her friend, escaped his cage and ate most of the woman's face and hands.

Likewise, much of Texas's population resists anything resembling confinement. Those in political power resist what they see as invasive gun laws. They resist what they see as an invasion by Mexico. And resist a takeover strategy by the national government. Even today, a vocal minority of Texans believe the state is a sovereign nation. Yet their fellow citizens are Mexican American, are locked up on death row, are subject to bad health because of elected politicians. They are in a different jail, blamed, captured, bolted up to suit their fellow Texans, and they too resist. The two groups exist like a strand of cool flame, burning with resistance, reflected in a mirror.

Capturing the macaques in Kyoto began in February 1972. One hundred fifty-two were lured into cages with bait and then loaded onto a Japan Airlines cargo flight. One monkey died en route; another lost a toe.

They arrived in the blinding light of Laredo near the Mexican border. Released, they pattered around the bunkers of cottontails. Surrounding them were roadrunners, timber rattlesnakes, tarantulas, bobcats, armadillos, javelinas, and more than one hundred species of cactus. They were encircled by an electric fence ten thousand feet long and eight feet high. A few of the monkeys grabbed the wires and locked on, the volts pulsing through their fur, and attending researchers had to dislodge them.

Laredo is eight degrees closer to the equator than Kyoto. It has high temperatures regularly over a hundred. In their first summer, the macaques ate coyotillo berries, which contain a lethal neurotoxin that has no antidote. A few monkeys were dragged from their enclosure by bobcats and eaten. Some were bitten and killed by rattlesnakes. More than a few contracted screwworms. Dozens were devastated by "valley fever," caused by inhaling fungus spores directly from the alkaline soil.

The macaques were surrounded by sand, predators, barbed wire, and an environment as hostile and unfamiliar as a desolate moon. Within the first two years of Texas living, half of the transplanted troop had died.

By the late seventies, after six years shaded under mesquite trees, toiling on bare soil, eking out a living in the Laredo sun, the snow monkeys of Texas adapted.

Scientists observing the troop found it easier to note what flora the monkeys didn't try consuming. Cactus became a troop favorite, especially the succulent flower bulbs. The macaques took to climbing prickly pears, deftly clinging between the spines, ripping off new-grown pads, and eating them like potato chips.

Over the next two decades the troop's numbers swelled to five hundred, then six. Generations of macaques were born on Texas soil. They became bilingual. The troop developed verbal calls and barks for creatures and foods found in the new world, like "rattlesnake" and "cactus," that when recorded and played back home were nonsensical to the Old World cohort. The snow monkeys learned to speak the language of their new home.

However, despite their new abilities, the monkeys were "global vagabonds," and, as Zygmunt Bauman writes, vagabonds pushed out of their homes by modernity "won't stay in place for long, however strongly they wish to, since nowhere they stop are they likely to be welcome."

When the rancher Edward Dryden died, his widow reportedly instructed the scientists: "Get these stinking monkeys off the property." She didn't like, apparently, what Donna Haraway calls "the risk of an intersecting gaze" of species to species, captor to captured. Confined creatures and people are often seen as "out there." To have them "here" was too close.

Shuttling the monkeys around, the scientists pulled together funds and purchased land outside San Antonio. But twenty-three acres couldn't contain them. The monkeys dug. They stole cabbages. They climbed mesquite branches and delicately lowered themselves onto private property. Macaque males were witnessed climbing the charged fences, even while being electrocuted.

They snuck. They ate up bait and crapped in deer blinds. They clambered on people's houses. Chewed up porch swings. Killed a dog, allegedly. They broke into houses while people were gone. Scared cattle. Ate cooling pies. And laughed.

It is no mere cliché to say that Texans love to hunt. There are more guns here per capita than in any other state besides Alaska. The only large predator in Texas is the cougar. There are maybe five hundred in the state, but you can kill as many as you want at any time.

Soon after hearing complaints of the snow monkeys' antics, the Texas Department of Parks and Wildlife declared the monkeys an "exotic unprotected species." It was open season on macaques. Deer at least have a time in the year when they can't be exterminated.

Hunters poured into San Antonio asking for monkey hunting permits, which were not needed and did not exist. The simians were like a weed that could be uprooted, an undocumented laborer who could be deported. Shipped to this country, they had adapted to the ecosystem, and now they could be shot.

Just before the scientists argued for the monkeys' lives in Texas legislation, four monkeys were tricked with food into climbing outside an enclosure and were gunned down by a man or men holding shotguns. The monkeys were a family, two of the macaques lactating females. Their killers were variously linked to friends of friends (who some said were Danish) and were never found.

Texas media blared their demise in ink and over the airwaves. Maligned in life, in death the macaques became martyrs. Grandmothers decried the deed. Wayne Newton, on hearing the story, flew to San Antonio to sing a concert raising money for the troop. He cried when he broke from song to talk about the slaughtered.

The scientists successfully argued their case, and the Texas government ruled that the monkeys were not invasive but "livestock." Cows, after all, cannot be tricked and shotgunned, although they are ultimately of foreign origin and will occasionally roam the countryside damaging cars and mailboxes. Under Texas law, Penal Code Sec. 9.42, a Texan is within his rights "using deadly force against another to protect land or tangible, movable property."

Horses were once eradicated from North America, but it is now legal to open fire on a thief who wrangles an imported stallion. Pigs first came from China, as did chickens, yet they too can't be shot. Similarly, you can't, without payment, hunt one of the nearly two hundred species of exotic African or Asian game that live on safari ranches throughout Texas. These animals were brought over for zoos originally, and when the menageries went bankrupt, the animals were turned loose across the countryside. They trespassed, but landowners realized many fellow Americans would pay good money for a safari they could otherwise find only overseas.

So for the price of a new Audi, you can scope and snipe a Cape buffalo or saw the horns off a dead scimitar oryx, an animal that has gone extinct in its native home in the Sahara. You can milk a cow, break a mustang, fry a chicken, but if you shoot one, you can be shot or sent to jail.

The global elite's dream, Zygmunt Bauman writes, is that one day all the poor of the world, all the vagabonds and huddled masses and undocumented, slip suddenly and silently into the good night. The world, he notes, is becoming a penal system, or, if you include animals, a safari ranch.

Seeing primates reminds Texans of who they are, a look across evolution, across the geothermal pools at fellow bathers, a look across borders. As Jacques Derrida said, "The animal looks at us, and we are naked before it."

It is only when Texans own something, like the grandfatherly grins of old livestock, that they let it be something to them, that they can save it legally. But salvation is more than a term, it is about becoming one with ourselves.

After the macaque family was gunned down, Hall of Fame pitcher Nolan Ryan espied a scurrying simian on his ranch in South Texas. Confused as anyone who didn't know the monkeys' story, he asked around. When Texas Parks and Wildlife learned that Ryan, the strikeout sultan, was interested, they designated him their Snow Monkey Ambassador. The monkeys were still a nuisance across the Hill Country, and Texas Parks thought that Ryan, one of the most famous Texans, could help with the monkey trouble.

In 2008 he appeared on a much-listened-to sports talk show, The Ticket. A taped conversation reveals Ryan retelling his first encounter at the refuge. Driving in among the mesquite and cactus, a bewildered Ryan heard a rattling on the car's roof, and then on the hood. Soon the vehicle was carpeted with what he describes as thousands of monkeys, crying, squealing, jumping, and playing.

"It's kind of like one of those things you see in Africa," he said. "I reluctantly got out and . . . one of them jumped off the top of the truck onto my shoulder and was hanging on me. And I didn't know what to do. I was like petrified wood."

Eventually, with the aid of Hershey's Kisses, Ryan won over the macaques. The chocolate, which since 1907 has won over children throughout the country, brought Ryan closer to the primate immigrants. Then scientists won over Ryan to the view that education was key, that Texans didn't know why the monkeys were here, why they were forced out of their home, why they had to adapt and respond to the harsh life they found. And thus the Hall of Famer, a man with a world-record 5,714 strikeouts, looked up to by a generation of Little Leaguers, became the monkeys' advocate.

The culmination of Ryan's ambassadorship was a series of Rangers games in which the ball team gave away thousands of furry gray stuffed dolls with twinkling eyes to spread awareness. July 1, 2012, was the first official Nolan Ryan Snow Monkey Day at Rangers Ballpark in Arlington. The first ten thousand children aged thirteen and under got a free monkey. At break time during the game, fans were asked to hold their livestock high up into the afternoon light, as everyone in the stadium stopped what they were doing.

The ten thousand children held up their gifts, which from far away, if you didn't argue with yourself, looked like infants gazing into the sun.

Uncle Shark

If I could remember just one piece of time from a recent trip to the Philippines, a month lavished with brightly memorable moments, it would be diving my face beneath the sea green and opening my eyes in terror.

Even though I was born near the ocean, I was raised and lived most of my life on West Texas cotton fields, nourished by a depleting aquifer, distinguished by dust storms, water shortages, desert beetles, and cactus for a west garden. The closest ocean was a nine-and-a-half-hour drive, which isn't bad for most people but is just enough that you wouldn't go down on a weekend. And if you were like me, you wouldn't go down at all.

I am terrified of the ocean now. The ocean is the biggest and most unpredictable body of water. It is the strange uncle who lives in a shack that is on stilts for some reason in your grandfather's backyard. You know he has a shotgun. Maybe you haven't seen it, but you've heard it, or heard of it, and it is all the scarier for the mystery.

My mother at the age of sixteen saw a shark fin when she was in an inflatable boat with her aunt outside Corpus Christi, Texas. The shark, a mako, brushed their dinghy, its skin like sandpaper, rough enough to pop the rubber surely, making squealing noises like baby screams on the tubes three times. The women paddled softly to shore, one using a tiny paddle while the other watched for fins, until they touched sand—and then they ran, churning the water, letting go of the raft so it flew away down the beach and was never seen again.

I saw *Jaws* when I was six after hearing my mom's story, and the movie let me wet my bed at night with a new excuse. For the longest time I never watched past the scene where the boy Alex Kintner, in his little red swim trunks like mine, is eaten on a rectangular floating tube like the kind I used to swim with. One time I came into my brother's room while he was watching the movie. (Unfazed, delighted at the gore, he asked our parents to rent the film some dozen times when we were young.) I stayed to watch, and when the shark hunter Quint got killed, caught in the maw as big as a steamer trunk, I knew the shark was motorized, its skin rubber, but that didn't matter. The imagination is powerful in the way it can turn the improbable, the inanimate, even the impossible into blood-soaked reality. Around this time I would go swimming in the community pool and would tear out of the water after a leap from the high dive, convinced a mad scientist or disgruntled lifeguard would raise a wall in the poolside revealing Jaws coming for me in my red swim trunks.

After I was about nine, I didn't swim in an ocean again until I was much older, twenty-four, and was in New Zealand. My teenage years had found the mountains of Colorado and the calm rivers of central Texas to be inviting scenery, free of fish bigger than my thigh.

At twenty-four I swam, but only in waters close to shore, and then where I could touch bottom, and I asked, of course, first about the local aquatic fauna.

But when I went snorkeling for the first time in my life in the pea green waters of the Philippines on a school trip as a grad student, I had to remind myself this wasn't a movie, that even if there were sharks around, they were a treasure to admire, a fascination to watch unfold. If I could, I tried to tell myself, I would want to touch one. That first day, when my breath slowed and my heart settled into its normal pattern, I admired the rock and the sea flora with the eyes of one who likes the natural world, knowing that the species and diversity on a coral reef are unparalleled. And even though this was secondary coral—dynamiting poachers killed off the original many years ago—there was still a circus of life: sea slugs

and salamander-looking things, anemones, parrot fish, and guppies swimming in schools the size of a bathtub, pulsating with the
waves, rolling underneath the surface in time with my own slowed-
down and assured heart.

And I thought of something: we are all from the water. Our species is only the distant cousin of those guppies and slugs and sea
snakes and even coral. Trace us back far enough and you find us a
lightning bolt in the ocean, some proteins that got together to form
amino acids, then some fish, and then you and me. Our fingers,
when they are wet, resemble the brain coral. We hiccup because our
lungs think we are returning to the sea. Our eyes still need salt water. We are living, breathing, walking memories and reflections of
the Precambrian. The flash of life, the spark of the universe.

Sharks of course are distant relatives. They are called primitive,
but really they are just older, closer to that first flame. And what
does it mean to be the same kind of fish or family member doing
the same thing for more years than we could count in the order of
a life, and still thriving? Sharks are beautiful tropes, unparalleled
predators; they help the ocean by keeping its species in check. They
define the sea with their fins breaking water, with their snouts always on the move, and with their seagull-shaped, telling grins.
They have eyes the color of the ocean at night.

They are, however, still pretty fucking scary. So when, my mind
playing tricks, I saw a shadow amid the sand and coral as a tropical storm far offshore stirred up the waves of the Philippine Sea and
they crashed overhead, I bolted for the beach. Then I thought better of it, as I knew from nature shows and conversation and, yes,
Jaws that swimming like a fish in distress is ringing the dinner bell.
So I went against the impulse and treaded water, calmly, trying to
imagine I lived there like a shrimp or a floating piece of seaweed,
uncaring for the mysteries and imagination below. Then my toes hit
sand, and then I went running up the surf, churning the water, conscious of the Filipino men and boys, shirtless, their hair salted, who
were smoking and taking a break from fishing, the boys, in blue
and black swim trunks, all laughing at me.

The Limbic System Roundup

On a seventy-degree Saturday in mid-March, at the dusty north end of Sweetwater, Texas, an unblemished cobalt sky hangs over the Nolan County Coliseum. Circling the rodeo arena are villages of bounce castles, portable rock-climbing walls, and retired veterans soliciting people to pay for parking. A man says to his girlfriend, "Did I hear someone say 'funnel cake'?" In front of me pass copious strollers among a mostly white cowboy-and-heavy-metal crowd: sleeve-cut-off rock T-shirts, tattoos, boots. Neighboring the coliseum are a popular flea market, a cook-off, a gun and knife show.

Inside the coliseum, at the center of the vortex, wriggle five thousand pounds of rattlesnakes.

This is what is known as the the World's Largest Rattlesnake Roundup. For the last fifty-nine years the festival has ferreted out around a thousand snakes every year. If the average length of a western diamondback, the most frequently caught, is four feet, you have almost a mile's worth of rattlers, squirming, coiling, striking, and tasting the sweat-filled air.

The snakes are why I've journeyed here. Since I was a child I have always wanted to peer into gross mortality—the maw of a shark, the gruesome decapitation of train wreckage, the fiery tongue of lava that licks out in Hawai'i. A mess of rattlesnakes is just another promised glimpse of mortality. As if, by peering over the edge, I might see all the way down.

Also, recently a venerable East Coast publication ran a scathing condemnation of the Sweetwater Roundup. But the writer hadn't even traveled to the Texas fête to see for herself that which she was earnestly snapping at. I decide to make my own foray into the snake pits.

There are dozens of theories about humans' fear of snakes. Such as, we evolved in trees where serpents would climb, and it would make sense to be snake-squeamish.

There's another theory that the fear is simply handed down, like DNA, an archaic notion of defending turf, an accumulation of generations. Snakes were a threat our ancestors had some control over on the chaotic plains, where wind, drought, fires, tornadoes, hail, and surprise visits from frost could only be endured. A struggling human is often bent upon exercising the little scratch of power he or she has.

The theory I'm most drawn to is that we fear serpents because we recognize in them our own limbic system. A biologist might scoff at this, but I, at least, like the metaphor even if its factual veracity is slippery. The limbic is the layer of the brain that goes deep beyond memory or reflection, what the editor of the *Neuropsychotherapist* has called "the centre for emotional responsiveness." Fight or flight, sleep or eat—that prehistoric survival strategist has kept our ancestors reproducing for eons. This part of our brain is triggered before the frontal lobe can process and will set us in a sweat, bolt us into a trot, or throw our hands up, fists curled—gut reactions we sometimes cannot anticipate. Lightning-fast synapses will circulate from sense organs to limbic to muscles to emotions. Our logic comes to the party quite late.

It's possible, just possible, that the limbic system response, that fight-or-flight mode, is roughly the constant awake state that a rattler lives with. Our dread, then, is that we can never escape—that curled up within our skulls lies a snake. A fear of the fangs within.

So far, it is a light day, only a few hundred people in the roundup, compared to the masses that will crowd around on Saturday, up to fifty thousand for the weekend. As I walk into the stadium, I reach down to touch the coliseum's dirt floor, finding it warm and beaten by years of bull hooves and mustangs. There are vendors of rattle-snake paraphernalia horseshoeing the arena. For sale: snakeskin boots, snake key chains, aluminum snake-catchers, snakeskin po-nytail holders, rattlesnake cowboy hats, stuffed rattlesnakes in per-petual attack poses, wallets for men and women, snake heads pre-served in jars, and rattlesnake "skin tanning solution."

A middle-aged man walks around poring over the vended goods. He looks out of place, dressed head to toe in khaki, with a wide face, jowls, and Vulcan-like ears. He glances at me and smiles. "Kind of a weird deal, isn't it?" he says.

I laugh, I expect him to go on about the snake tanning oil, but he says, "You know, being cruel to animals? Of course, the hillbillies don't care; they just catch a bunch of snakes and make money."

To be courteous, I assent. He pauses, eyes on mine, seeming to want to talk more, but I don't engage him. He shrugs and wanders away. The truth is, I haven't made up my mind. I pause at the cli-chéd, othering word "hillbilly," and what the man thought, and why he came here. What he says makes sense, I guess, but I won-der how much disgust is a function of the limbic, a gut reaction to a coiled serpent or to a group of West Texans decapitating them.

I round a corner of booths, and I see that Monique Evans, Miss Texas 2014 (so reads her sash), is here. She dons her sequined ti-ara, posing in front of a cowboy-booted Jaycee who hangs a gap-ing western diamondback over her shoulder. Evans is inordinately tan, with an oval face and dark eyes. She performs a kind of smile-scowl, her head cocked just so, peering at the fanged reptile held in midair. The snake is a foot from her frosty smile, its jaws opening and closing. If there was ever a time for Evans's limbic system to fire, this would be it.

Several people snap photos, but then I notice many of them ig-noring Evans in favor of what's behind her. At the back corner of the arena is an octagonal enclosure fashioned of chainlink and Plexiglas, thirty feet in diameter, filled with a mass of terrified, slithering flesh. This is where the rattlesnakes arrive. The snake holding pit. Two twenty-something Jaycees, decked in rawhide leggings and steel-toed boots, wade inside, knee deep in the rattlers, a swirl of animated, speckled diamonds. The snakes are wrapping around each other, nipping at hindquarters to secure a better space in the arena lights. The Jaycees gently scoot aside piles of snakes with their armored boots. They slosh through the serpents. The snakes rise up like waves. They are, despite popular discourse, gentle.

To my right a wooden clacking noise. A pair of Jaycees outside the pit have tipped a box of snakes and are dumping them inside. The pine boxes are about four feet long and two feet wide with a trap door that flips open, so snakes rain into the pit, splashing at the Jaycees' boots. Another new box releases a fresh wave of serpents and hormones and feces. The snakes pile up like snowdrifts.

Staring at the one-ton quivering mass of rattlesnakes, I am mesmerized as if staring at a swimming pool bursting with sharks or a lightning bolt crawling out of the sky. I feel like a teenager doped on acid, hallucinating a wall come to life as terrifying, slithering things.

Also, the collective rattling from the pit, the buzzing, is the incessant humming of cicada armies in a forest, something organic but preternaturally unnerving. I can't turn away. And neither can a group of about thirty people gawking with me. We are drawn to the hypnotic tune.

In Texas, the western diamondback is the most abundant viper. It has diamond markings the length of its body but is more easily identified by its "coon tail," the black and white stripes below the rattle. No other creature has a rattler's warning call. In design, the rattle is not a maraca but linked sprockets that when shaken blur and clap. Each is made of keratin, the same substance as our fingernails and hair.

The western diamondback dines on tiny, unfortunate mammals, slow amphibians, eggs, and birds. It can live everywhere on land except in cities and where trees run amok. It avoids swamps, prefers rugged topography, thrives in the openness of a Pecos Valley or Llano Estacado. But it will make do with a trash heap or a barn.

Herpetologists widely believe the rattle evolved to ward off aimless fauna like bison. But if you are walking along an ancient creek, the most common way a snake will react to you is to lie still and blend with the geology. A rattler knows the craggy mass of sandstone and slate will protect it far better than two hollow fangs or a keratin rattle. If someone creeps close, the snake will try to squirm over a dune, through a crevice, inside a mouse hole. Backed against a wall, the snake will widen its tail into a base, the counterbalance of a mortar. The upper body will morph into an S coil, rising a foot off the ground. Meanwhile, the tail quivers.

If an adventurous man (for it's almost always men) takes another step or reaches a hand out, perhaps with a beer-inspired guffaw, he will look down and see two red eyes of blood peering out from above his ankle, or atop the stringier part of his hand. The man will feel inoculated, shotgunned. Blood will rush to his ears, and his pupils will dilate. He may break into a sweat as the sensation of a vise grip marches up his limb. He may see the withdrawing snake, the buzzing tail, and maybe a teardrop of rose glistening at the fangs' icicle tips.

Most people who get bit by diamondbacks have earned it.

Inside the measuring pit located next to the holding pit stands Terry Armstrong, a squat, jovial Jaycee dressed in a white button-up shirt and jeans. Above his round Irish face, red curls poke out of his cowboy hat. He is responsible for gauging snake vitals, one diamondback at a time. He peers over the lip of the pit's polyethylene walls and educates a young boy, also in cowboy hat: "You know what to do when you see one?" The boy shakes his head, open mouthed. Terry continues, "You stay very still and then slowly back away. It won't hurt you if you don't hurt it. Don't touch it. I tried catching one, one time, with my bare hands, and it damn near killed me."

Using the standard two-foot-long metal claw, Terry hooks an agitated rattler that fires out toward his ankles. On the table, Terry lays the snake out and with his snake-catcher's hook pinches the snake's head against the wood. By hand he grabs the skull and underside of the jaws, forcing the fangs to open, venom milkable, as the tail twitches around his arm.

Later Terry leaves the pit to talk. He is shorter than he seemed handling the coiled ropes of toxin, and he talks 190 words a minute. Twice before, Terry was in charge of the roundup. Now he maintains a, quote, "influential" position.

The talk quickly turns to activists who want to shut the roundup down. "A lot of them we call 'herpers,'" short for herpetologists, he tells me, and chuckles. "I've gotten all kinds of threats from them, including on my life."

Apparently, though, for their pains, the activists have influenced Terry. "We used to do all that bad stuff," he says, referring to pouring straight gasoline into snake burrows to catch them, spinning snakes in canvas bags, prodding and beating snakes into racing each other, sewing rattlesnake mouths shut for family photos. "But I was young then," he says.

"I really like rattlesnakes," he says fervently. "I really admire them. And we're not hurting them that much. What we kill every year isn't even what cars on Texas roads kill. The same nests we hunt always supply snakes next year."

I ask why the activists don't leave him alone.

"They're really upset at the killing. But we only kill about a half. The other we sell to dealers."

"Like who?" I ask.

He points at the vendors.

"For wallets and belts?"

"Yeah," he says, and wheezes as if he hadn't thought about what it takes to make snake apparel before.

Then he says something I think hits out from his soul: "Man, this is our town, this is our livelihood. You see how many people come here every year? We make our money off this. We need this."

The thing that gets me is not the killing at the roundup but that many of the snakes released and beheaded in the arena have been sleeping and suffering in crates for weeks or maybe months at a time. Some caught snakes die before they get to the arena. How much do snakes suffer? Even a limbic system trapped in the dark to shit itself must be screaming on some level.

But the problem with this condemnation is that it leaves out the complexity of the human-animal drama, the fact that my hands were already bloody before coming over to the arena. And have been bloody at least since humans wiped out many species of megafauna pecking their way around the globe.

There has never been an Edenic communion between humans and animals. I've often heard fellow eco-writers and eco-warriors claim it's because we're out of touch with "nature" that we wreak harm on other species. Largely I find that sentiment simplistic. It elevates us humans past the eating, shitting, tribalizing animals that we are. Sometimes I wonder if what our frontal lobes do is justify gut instinct, our occasional wantonness, our limbic desire.

Which is certainly not a new observation. In 1826 the British essayist William Hazlitt in his seminal work "On the Pleasures of Hating" wrote his thoughts about a spider for which he felt "a sort of mystic horror and superstitious loathing." He believed then that civilization *should* be advanced enough that we didn't have to enact violence on all things that frightened us. But really he was skeptical of the progression of the animal mind. He believed humans were perpetual cave people, acting out primal aggression.

Currently, I don't know if we're any different. We flock to witness fires, crane our necks for human spaghetti on highways, kill things for sport. We click on videos showing reporters shot on TV, montages of train crashes, a pigeon exploding in midair as a pitcher throws an ill-timed fastball. "The wild beast resumes its sway within us," Hazlitt wrote, "and as the hound starts in his sleep and rushes on the chase in fancy, the heart rouses itself in its native lair, and utters a wild cry of joy, at being restored once more to freedom and lawless, unrestrained impulses."

A few families gather around the arena's central demonstration pit, and dozens of rattlers echo together from within like the muted pitch of a waterfall. David Sager, with a microphone clipped to his shirt, walks into the pit, which is sort of like an above-ground swimming pool, surrounded on all sides by wooden bleachers coated in decades of hoof-tossed dirt. Unlike the other

Jaycees with their leg armor, Sager wears only jeans, his hat, and a Coors logo patch on his pressed white shirt. Sager appears stiff and walks laboriously as his two-packs-a-day voice drones out over the stadium.

It's only the first day, but already the demonstration pit reeks with a swampy odor, the rust-yellow crust of snake feces pooling on the ground.

Back in 1950s, Sweetwater was a nest of snakes, Sagar tells us. Diamondbacks, he says, came into town because of dryness. They came to the city looking for succor. Sweetwater's only goal, Sager says, was not to step into rattlers.

Sager hooks a large diamondback with his snake-catcher and lays it on the table in the center of the ring. Another Jaycee hands him a balloon: long, pink, and phallic, the tip decorated with a Sharpie smile. Sager tickles the reptile with the balloon. The snake rises, licks the air. Sager nudges it again with the inflated phallus-face, and the diamondback fires. The pink balloon explodes, sending a sharp gasp through the arena.

"The only reason a snake will strike you is for food or self-defense," Sager reminds us. No one is able to change what it is, he warns. "You can't defang a rattlesnake. Within an hour, he'll already have another fang going, and within a day, he can bite again."

It's not that a fang grows rapid-fire, but that fangs are always already there. Backup. Behind each fang a series of developing replacements. Fangs all the way down.

Sager leaves the snake alone for about ten minutes, discussing diamondbacks and the history of Sweetwater, boring the audience, some of whom scoot away. But then, suddenly, he reaches toward the rattler, which has coiled inside the mass of its body, and slides it off the table onto his other hand. He balances the mass on his palm, circling the pit like a waiter with a dessert tray, the handheld coiled snake raised for the crowd to see. "They're really not aggressive creatures," he explains, "except the mothers when they have young. The rest of the time, they're as passive as a refrigerator."

He circles the demonstration pit, holding out the tamed predator, the biblical monster, so defenseless-seeming, perched on an aging man's naked hand. "I think they're here for a purpose," he says. "God put them here, like all things."

I walk away feeling a shiver of disassociation. Snakes are God's creatures, so they're beheaded by the thousands? But then maybe Sager doesn't agree with all that's going on and this is his form of protest while remaining in-group. Also people slaughter millions of animals for food and probably think they're here for a reason too. Maybe the gulf between Edenic creation and mass slaughter is formed by how we view other animals as things and ourselves as not-animals.

The relationship between man and snake has been tenuous in America, at least since the massive arrival of Europeans in the 1600s. As early as 1680, settlers had initiated gore-a-thons on many creatures: mountain lions, bears, wolves, sharks. Around 1740, many communities set aside specific days for slaughter, like a government holiday.

The events drew crowds. Before home entertainment, snake roundups allowed congregations of picnic-goers to witness National Geographic–like bloodiness. There were rattlesnake shootings, decapitation contests, stomping challenges. But the events were all bootstrap. In 1939 the first official celebration of reptile violence sprung up in Okeene, Oklahoma, which is still running the world's oldest roundup. Though more modest now, in the 1950s it drew almost a hundred thousand people each year, multiplying the town's population a hundredfold.

With the popularity of Okeene, roundups popped up in states ranging from Oklahoma to Pennsylvania to Florida to South Dakota. As rural populations fell, the bloodlust wore off or was sublimated on TV. Now there are only a handful around the country—one in Alabama, one in Georgia, a few in Texas and Oklahoma. There are no rattlesnake roundups left in any of the other historical roundup states. Sweetwater still claims to be the largest.

I kind of doubt the ostensible explanation for the Sweetwater Roundup. Sure, people don't want their ankles poisoned, but they also want bloodiness and a reason to have a town gathering. In this way I don't think they're much different from sports towns.

One could argue that modern gladiators have choices, unlike snakes, but I'm not so sure. My father did sportswriting for a decade and saw the lack of options for many impoverished players who were brutalized for spectators. This is why he barred me from football. And the question here is not of scale but of arena.

Also, cattle and chickens and pigs and turkeys are butchered every day after suffering confinement, many of them for America's comfort food, cooked in bloody ritualistic events called barbecues. The appetite for blood is widespread. It would seem unfair to single out one community in Texas, when the core of the problem edges back into the human mind. And more, is supported by the culture at large, by ESPN and the Food Network. Fifty thousand people, after all, is half the capacity of many football stadiums.

Sometimes I wonder if opening up slaughterhouses to public viewing would be beneficial. Or if ESPN followed around injured players who did not make it. For us to see what goes on behind the curtain, what feeds us, body and soul, what makes us a nation, a people, a species, a loosely connected network of communities, many of which pride themselves on legitimized-though-objectively-questionable activities.

After David Sager's show winds down, a mechanical snapping sound punctuates the air. I walk back toward the holding area, from which the sound issues, and find that killing and skinning pits have materialized, quickly constructed with cattle guard barriers. Six teenage Jaycees, five male and one female, outfitted in chest aprons and gloves, are working in an assembly line above wheeled-in steel sinks. Each dangles a beheaded snake from a wire. The reptiles are gutted, fluids spilling into the drains below, and skinned.

Everyone, for twenty dollars, can gut and skin their own western diamondback too and take the hide for a souvenir. The first customers I see are a bewildered pink-shirted ten-year-old girl and a buff, blond, twenty-something man in pressed khakis, loafers, and Polo—casual business attire that he'll soon regret wearing.

The pair skin their snakes with an attendant Jaycee in camouflage coveralls. The Jaycee uses a Bowie knife to slice up the length
of the snake's dangling stomach. The casual-biz man reaches in on
command, pulling out the bloated purple guts, splashing life juice
onto his pants. Both man and girl detach the innards and let them
drop into the bucket at their feet. After a few moments of panic, the
man lets the Jaycee finish the skinning while he stares forlornly at
his clothes. The Jaycee tugs on the hide; it comes off like a Popsi-
cle wrapper. The girl stares wide-eyed and quiver-lipped at the once
live thing's unpackaging.

Afterwards, both customers spread the harvested skins for a
smile-less photograph. Their hands still coated in viscera, they
walk to the white butcher paper hanging from the arena seats behind them and plant their palms, soaked bloody, against the wall.
After washing, they will sign their names below their red hand-
prints.

Much like the rattling from the holding pit had done earlier, the
sound of a periodic piston firing that feels much closer now has
deafened me. I see that on the other side of the skinning pit two
men are at work decapitating. One man is short, bald, bespecta-
cled, and owns a face like Ben Kingsley's. He reaches into a large
trashcan with an aluminum claw-hand snake-catcher to retrieve a
twitching viper. Then he lays it out on a three-foot stump, the snake
rattling and gaping and hissing. The second man, the executioner,
a tall, large-bodied Latino with a ten-gallon straw hat, leans over it
with a Craftsman nail gun in his left hand. The floor beneath their
feet is spattered with patterns the shape and color of autumn leaves.

The executioner places the nail gun barrel against the reptile
head. Pulls the trigger. A pop ensues, and he moves the gun away.
There are no nails, just the little bolt that, as quick as venom, burrows into the reptile's brain. The head and body twitch until the
nail-gun man swings a machete with his right hand, which severs
the snake head. The jaws are left thrashing on the stump. The body
gets thrown into a bucket, the tail twitching as it slips over the lip
and into the pile of bodies.

Several children are watching with Keanu-Reeves-in-The-Matrix expressions. Most are awed, but one little boy, who can't stop shaking his leg, looks up in frenzied delight at a particular gruesome decap, sprayed viscera, muscle tendons exposed and dripping. The boy shrieks and then espies the buckets of heads. "The heads are still moving!" he yells at his dad, who stands petrified in his boots, his hand on the boy's scalp, frozen. The boy repeats, "They're opening and closing still!" Indeed, I peer over, past the terrified man, to see the jaws still biting as if they could still defend their now separated bodies.

The executioner's eyes have the half-sleepy at-work look of a longhaul truck driver. The bite of his machete into wood is damped and earthy. The compressed-air shock of the nail gun is sharp, unmuted, clearly puncturing the atmosphere of the arena. Strange what I'm finding humane.

When the killing team takes a break, I ask the volunteer machete swinger what his job is like. He wipes his brow under his huge floppy hat and says, in a southern accent, "It's like a family reunion. I've been doing this every year for fifteen years. It's like hunting, only here we hunt snakes too. People meet up, have fun. It's a good time."

I ask him why the nail gun and the redundant decap, and he says that they used to only swing machetes, to separate fangs from bodies, but animal rights groups grew vociferous.

"The nail gun is less painful?" I ask.

"Supposedly." He shrugs.

"Do you like this"—I gesture at the killing floor—"or hunting better?"

"All of it," he replies. "It's like deer season. You get some boys together, go hunting, come back, do some skinning."

I tell him I was just thinking it's something along the lines of fishing, and he nods, smiles. With fishing, which I too enjoy, there's the cruel catching, the gutting, the skinning, the beheading, the twitching, the eventual lifelessness. Same with lobster cracking. I don't look at the executioner other than as someone engaged in a mildly satisfying hobby as an excuse to hang with friends who legitimize what he does. Though the crowd brings this activity into the realm of spectacle, talking with him makes it feel intimate, a routine pastime.

I do wonder why they have to kill *all* the snakes here, and I ask him. He shrugs again. "Snakes get in people's way," he says, though halfheartedly, like he really doesn't want to think about the answer. I don't press him. Just as I don't question myself too hard about last night's hamburger dinner. Also, he picks up his blood-caked machete and is more than a little intimidating.

As the men resume their killing, I'm not sure what to do here. I'm awed by the raw power of that much coiled fury, yet empathetic about the confinement and execution. I'm bewildered by some of the children taking this all in with glee. I'm encouraged to find that most adults, while wide-eyed at their first brush with snake death, grow weary, appear nauseated, and stroll off.

It's an odd congruity, the ritualistic and yet mechanistic slaughter coupled with a clear message from both Terry Armstrong and David Sager that these creatures are harmful if provoked. It's also perfectly predictable that if you have a group of friends who enjoy doing something and need an excuse to get together, they will keep doing it, especially if a crowd of fifty thousand validates it.

Why else would American college football be so popular with the grown men who dress in ridiculous outfits, drink copiously, and watch young players enact their beloved bloody sport? Young men who often get hurt on the entertainment battlefield, who spend their college years pursuing promised but implausible fantasies? It's not just the individual brain, after all, that excuses the limbic system.

Later, Miss Texas stands in front of the skinning pit signing autographs, posing, and answering questions. Behind her hang seven nooses covered in blood, used to hold up snakes in mid-skinning. As she laughs, waves, and signs, half a dozen Jaycees, all of them young, most of them in plaid, go about butchering the day's kill.

They string up the headless snakes, scissor open their bellies, disembowel them, and with a few cuts and finger work, slide the skins off. They hold the (on average) four-foot-long, eight-inch-wide skins behind Miss Texas, sometimes flanking her with hides. They tack several big ones to the white wall. They occasionally leave bloody fingerprints. Miss Texas waves at her fans, and the gory walls, signed by children, wave too.

Becoming Mascot

Growing up in West Texas, I was the son of a sportswriter, and our college team, Texas Tech, had two mascots, a Zorro-masked rider aboard an all-black stallion and a Yosemite Sam ripoff named Raider Red. The latter was seven feet tall, sporting a flaming handlebar mustache and two scarlet geysers of eyebrows. He swaggered around the edges of Jones Stadium, thumbs in his belt, picking up phallic hand cannons that belched when the team scored. His dull eyes and morose grin registered satisfaction whether the team won or lost.

Yet the gun-toting Warner Brothers plagiarist was not controversial; the horse was. Tech had the audacity to let a woman ride in 1974, generating the most hate mail in the school's history. They also let their stallion gallop after touchdowns despite the danger presented by three hundred people crisscrossing the sidelines.

Lately I've been remembering this horse and thinking about mascots and why we choose to cover ourselves with animals. What is it about the animal that is central to violent sport?

FIRST QUARTER

When I was a boy, I admit to a thrill when seeing Tech's horse gallop, the creases of its equine muscles, the cold black kill in its eyes. The stallion could stir you even from across the sea of screaming fans. In the lower sections where I sat, you could feel your seat shake as he ran. The hooves beat in your chest. The horse was a fulcrum of the team, the locus for the identity of millions of students and alumni who were standing in the bleachers or watching at home, their index finger and thumb spread out for the "guns up" for Tech, their yelling, tribal warfare.

Ignoring the danger, Tech continued to allow its horse to circle the field, and in 1982 the stallion bowled over an SMU pom-pom girl who spent a week in the hospital with injuries to her head, face, jaw, teeth, and legs. She later sued the college and won an undisclosed amount. Another year, the horse knocked a referee unconscious.

In 1993 a female rider of a young horse named Double T fell when her new saddle slipped. Double T, masterless, cantered down the sideline, hooves clattering as he aimlessly circled the turf. Confused at the end zone when he wasn't pulled up, Double T turned onto the ramp where the opposing team had its locker rooms. He slipped; witnesses say his feet "flew out from under him." He tumbled and knocked his head against a wall and fell dead beneath the scoreboard.

I was in my usual seat when it happened, across the field, age ten, foam red "guns up" on my right hand, black and red camouflage on my face. I noticed only when it was all over: the rider crying, Double T neck-broke, tongue hanging out, blood on the wall. The horse had slid down the ramp to the sewer grates where sweat and dew collect. Someone had covered him with a tarp.

Like many Americans, I harbored some Disneyfied hope of a resurrection. I assumed trusty Double T would rebound, four-legged kung-fu-film-like. Or maybe he would be cheered as fallen linemen are, limping to the sidelines or carried out in a stretcher to an ambulance.

I remember thinking at one point, *Why doesn't he just get up already?* It was the same annoyance I had sometimes when players went down, when those with joint sprain or concussion were borne away, holding up a drive. I felt what might be an all-too-common obsession with the game's unfolding. The players, like the horse, were characters on a stage housing the drama of the field and, when injured, had worn out their parts. A ten-year-old doesn't worry if

those players can afford knee surgery or if they lose their scholar-
ships and end up in fast food service.

When I was a teenager, I saw a man folding my sandwich at a
Schlotzsky's with a National Championship ring on his finger. I
asked, and he said he'd played for Nebraska. I was naively stunned,
never expecting to see a player doing anything but carrying the football or blocking the line or maybe, when he was older, announcing
a game. When players left the field, if they weren't in the business,
it was as if they didn't exist.

When Double T died, Texas Tech won by a single touchdown,
and it was a harbinger of a winning season. The team triumphed,
and I imagined I'd see Double T back under the saddle, the bit in
his mouth, ready to celebrate. Then, one game at night, with a dewy
sheen on his forelegs and stomach and his jet black coat matching
the sky, he was. The new Double T was a second string named High
Red, who himself would die three summers later. Spooked by lightning in his pasture, the horse would run into a fence and impale his
heart on a picket.

I learned about High Red's death from my father, who wasn't going to write about it in the newspaper he worked for. In the impres-
sionable way of adolescents, I developed a sense that you don't talk
about those who have left the field. That the game is the thing, the
relentless pressing forward of brackets and stats and fourth-quar-
ter charges. The game itself gallops on.

SECOND QUARTER

I'm thirty-five now, and because I live in Texas again, I sometimes
have to debate the validity of college and pro sports' existence for
their brainlessness and time-waste and predation on young ambi-
tion. But when a game is on a TV within the corners of my vision, I
will turn and stare like a hungry dingo. A friend of mine who studies
anthropology explained it this way: when our *Homo erectus* ancestors
detected a commotion in the shadows or a flame across the hill, it
behooved them to pay attention. A fight or a light could yield food,
maybe some bones for tools. Or the rustling could come your way
and arrive in the form of a long-fanged tiger. So whenever a game is

on and the screen is floating in my view, forgive me if I'm harping on anthropology to explain a shortcoming, I will watch. Even less valorized sports like curling. I have become enthralled with curling.

My wedding anniversary sometimes falls on Superbowl Sunday, and in 2014 my partner and I went to an upscale sushi restaurant, but not even there could we escape the Bruce Willis commercials, the painted chests, the Doritos, the cleavage. The game was on six television screens above the sushi bar, and as the master chef cut octopus tentacles, he was lamenting the shame of the Broncos, who were losing very badly. I found this pleasing at the time; for some reason I desired the Broncos decimated, though I didn't know why. It wasn't like I had a stake in the game or that I watched football or knew anything about any of the players except Peyton Manning, who was running down his twilight.

My partner was happy that I mostly paid attention to things other than the screens, that I *ate* rather than inhaling our food, which she, a Japanese native, commented was the best sushi she'd had yet in the States. Still, even when the Broncos began losing by five touchdowns, I found it hard to peel away my gaze. I wanted the slaughter. Yumiko said my eyes were drooling.

Some historians have argued that football is a manifestation of a war zone, a four-down, end-zone land grab. When a player spikes the ball, he is also, in some sense, claiming a nest. Maybe this is why I wanted the Broncos to lose. Too close to my own mascot, they were making me peer at myself and my biology. I, and many viewers, experience sports astride a mental mascot, galloping, flying, or stampeding into combat. Humans haven't evolved away from our origins in this view; the fangs and webbed feet remain.

All this to say, I support a system that is gladiatorial. I acknowledge that it's the disenfranchised populations who enact violent sports in our collegiate arenas for no pay, while an absurdly rare few become role models (and some of them very *bad* role models). I know all this and yet feel the rush of the forward pass, imagine the air between the basketball and the fabric as the net goes "tshuuck," hear the uncanny ecstasy in the announcer's furor when a FIFA-approved orb sails past the gloves of a leaping goalie.

When the fans next to me erupt in unmitigated pandemonium, I glide into the glory of sports because it's there. It's obtainable. You can say this team won this at this time. I can't even tell you if organizing my e-mail, getting through to my insurance company finally, and grading essays today was a victory or not. I don't know who my opponent is. A score gives me the clear assurance so fleeting in the quotidian push of pen across paper and the folds of laundry and the ceaseless cries of shopping lists.

HALFTIME

But who wins best mascot, I've wondered—a childish, childhood-originated idea, though expected in a hierarchical arena. As a kid, I remember arguing who could beat up whom, the mounted horse or the longhorn? These elementary school debates were serious, and during the year when Notre Dame blasted Florida State from number one, my friends and I fought about how tough Irishmen must be if bare-fisted leprechauns could vanquish a warrior tribe.

For a child, what other reality exists as an explanation for the seeming randomness of success? In this way we argued about whose father could pummel whose, whose mother was prettier, whose older sibling was faster. I grew up inside the brackets of a little-league life status tournament. I didn't, and still don't, really, want to be anything but holding the trophy for World's Best Human.

And so came from my perpetual self-doubt a perennial posing of myself above others, if only in my brain. I still find it difficult to wiggle away from this gaze. Even when talking to those who are older, who are sharper-witted, and even those I could only logically conclude are my equals, my mind finds a way out of being the lesser, as if there were only two options. As if the universe operates like a coin, one face beneath the other.

My vote, though, is for Sammy the Slug, of the University of California, Santa Cruz. Sammy resembles a flattened rabbit crossbred with an orc baby and dyed vanilla-pineapple. Slugs are shell-less mollusks that thrive on redwood forest floors. The banana variety has been a mascot of UCSC since the 1960s.

By a ratio of phallus size to body, banana slugs have some of the largest in the world. Their members can grow as large as 75 percent of their bodies. And they are hermaphroditic. Each slug has a fully functioning penis as well as ovaries. After having sex, which the slugs will do copiously throughout the year, they sometimes eat each other's nutrient-rich cocks to aid in the production of eggs.

According to Slugweb, Sammy represents "many of the strongest elements of the campus: contemplation, flexibility, non-aggressiveness and, perhaps above all, an iconoclastic challenge toward the status quo." Sammy has gone on to win *Reader's Digest*'s "Best Mascot," the National Directory of College Athletics' "Best College Mascot," and *Sports Illustrated*'s "Nation's Best College Nickname."

I can't stop from asking, what does it mean to have an award-winning, "official" iconoclast mascot who lets its lover eat its penis? Ironic that in the college sports world, which favors tenacity and ferocity and violence, the slug has whipped the tiger, the bear, and all others. That a ground-dwelling, spineless creature wins the member-measuring contest.

THIRD QUARTER

Most of America, of course, prefers mascots that can disembowel an opponent or at least debark a tree. Some schools are even bold enough to bring these wild creatures onto the field—North Carolina its big-horned ram, LSU a live Bengal tiger, Colorado its buffalo, Baylor its bear, and Georgia its pampered bulldog, Uga, who has bitten the legs of rival players.

Mascotting can be serious despite its relegation to the sidelines. The Stanford Redwood, for instance, was kidnapped by the "Phoenix Five" and held for ransom for five days. The Detroit Tiger PAWS was sued for "distracting" a fan who was hit in the face by a foul ball. The Philadelphia Phillies' very furry and phallic green Phanatic (who doesn't wear pants) once got a beating from Los Angles Dodgers manager Tommy Lasorda. Wild Wing from the Anaheim Ducks failed to bounce on a trampoline and arc through a ring of fire. He lodged a skate, fell face-first into the charring ring, and thus became duck flambé on ice.

Apart from Tech's horse, Yale's bulldog Handsome Dan VI reportedly had a heart attack from fright at game fireworks. Two of Navy's mascot goats, Bill XVI and Bill XVII, have died from eating grass treated with herbicides. Three of UConn's huskies named Jonathan have been killed by cars. In 1885, Tufts University's elephant was run over by a train and then stuffed and propped up outside the school.

But the most enlightening sacrifice of a mascot for its team, I think, comes from Bevo, the University of Texas's longhorn. Though Bevo is now cared for by a team of volunteers and has attended at least one presidential inauguration, the original Bevo was an afterthought.

In 1916 a leader of the alumni was working cattle rustler raids in Laredo for the U.S. attorney general and turned up a very large, very orange steer for sale. Though UT teams were called the Longhorns, they hadn't thought to bring a live creature to their sidelines. "Bevo" arrived, emaciated and carsick from 240 miles of travel without water, just in time for the Austin kickoff against the Texas A&M Aggies. The Longhorns won, 21–7, but this was Bevo's first and last game-day appearance.

A year later, the United States entered World War I. Sixty pounds of Bevo feed per day became exorbitant during wartime shortages, and the university also wanted to trim expenses. So Bevo was slaughtered, cooked, and served to University of Texas football players at the annual athletics banquet in 1920.

The other option, voted down by UT officials, was letting Bevo run around on campus to fend for himself. I love imagining that was an option in the 1920s, that a collegiate campus was a vote away from being overrun with livestock. It's like when I imagine, wistfully, the University of North Texas's eagle roosting atop the 125-year-old admin building or, perversely, Clemson's tiger running loose through urbanity, dining on street dogs.

Some psychologists have suggested our obsession with monsters stems from *not* having animals stalking us at night. Our safety feels unreal. With ferocious, furry, fanged mascots, maybe that's a part of what we're doing—putting the wild and unpredictable back into our lives.

In 2005 the NCAA began culling offensive mascots. Chief Illiniwek and Monty Montezuma got the ax; so too, deservedly, many Redskins.

Until 2010 the University of Mississippi's mascot was a goateed, finely dressed southern "planter" named Colonel Reb. I am awed that what appears to have been an obvious connection to slaveholding landed gentry served as a mascot well into the twenty-first century, at a school where African Americans made up 17 percent of the enrollment. After abandoning the "colonel," Ole Miss employed a black bear in a suit with a white hat.

According to ESPN.com, the black bear was not just a simple afterthought alternative, but connected to the university through William Faulkner. The bear in question, Old Ben from Faulkner's famous (long) short story "The Bear," is a persistent beast. Ben is ancient, sly, mysterious, tough, seemingly immortal, and ghostly. In the story, it takes a near-wild dog named Lion to sniff Old Ben down. Lion and Ben fight, and while the bear is disemboweling the hound, a hunter (soon to go insane) climbs atop Ben as if he were mounting a horse. Thus, the literary critic can read, the white man is taming wildness. The hunter slips a knife into Ben's rib cage. The bear dies, and the wilderness falls apart in the following years as logging companies move in and slash away. Only the squirrels are left and the same hunter breaking his gun on a tree trunk trying to claim them.

The University of Mississippi wants to "connect with its roots," they say. So, to this aim, they've covered their slave owner in fur and made a cursory connection to a depressing story of assimilation at the hands of a white man who goes crazy because of his deed.

A few years ago I had an Indian mascot conversation with my class. One student from D.C. began complaining about how President Obama had advocated nixing the Redskins.

"I mean, that's been my father's team for thirty years," he whined.

I could have incriminated this barely-adult adult in a long line of tyrannical white dudes who have occupied this nation, painted their faces, appropriated the other. I could have sneered, "Boy, thirty years, now that's a long time! Considering how long Native Americans have been here," and lost a student forever. Which is what I sometimes do. Imagining students as the "other" othering.

However, that day, in a clear-eyed way that is rare for me, I said, "Well, imagine if there were a team called the Wichita White Trash or the Cleveland Crackers." I also relayed how Sherman Alexie once asked a coliseum of Redskins, "What if your school was called the Environmentally Devastating White People?" As Alexie knew, perhaps, a lesson within a joke can sometimes get an eighteen-year-old grinning and reconsidering ear to ear, a magical thing taking shape before you.

In academia, I sometimes feel quarantined from reality. I lose sight that people usually grow up with what they are born to. My young student was inside "Redskin" territory not by right but by circumstance. But I can cut these buds, graft these human stalks, uproot entire beings, steal them from their nests and raise them. They'll sit in my lap and imprint like the first pet wolves.

But I must move people into their new selves with a quick laugh and a smile of recognition that I was born with mascots too—a West Texas white boy, a Red Raider.

The self is much less fully formed than I would have thought when I was younger. Growing up, I was fooled into believing that the human clay hardened. But now I've found I can sometimes peel off parts of myself, when provoked or cajoled or teased, rather than slaughtered and defeated, as easily as if they were pieces to a feathered costume.

FOURTH QUARTER

On the international scene, the World Cup mascot for Mexico in 1970 was a slant-eyed, sombreroed boy named Juanito with a midriff T-shirt over a prodigious belly. I can't imagine any country getting away with this now. Then again, a cubist Catalan sheepdog headlined the summer Olympics in Barcelona in 1992. Toronto is still the Maple Leafs. Youppi!, in a costume designed by the creator of Miss Piggy, became the mascot for the Montreal Expos for twenty-five years and then switched over to the Montreal Canadiens hockey team. One of the oldest soccer clubs in Thailand is called the Thailand Tobacco Monopoly, or TTM.

In 2008 at the Beijing summer games, among four other mascots, one was a giant panda named Jingjing. I bought a stuffed Jingjing for my then girlfriend, now wife, but the time I spent in Beijing was miserable. The air was saturated with particulate matter, and I got stomach-squeezing headaches. I was pickpocketed. I bunked in a hostel with a hard-drinking, foul-mouthed Aussie who vomited in the bathroom and didn't clean, slamming doors at early morning hours. There were no other rooms in the hostel. There were no other rooms in Beijing during the Olympics.

The Chinese had spent good money on the games, bulldozing old neighborhoods and lead-laden factories. Where those people went I don't know, but I stayed in one of the older parts of town that was still standing, with streets as wide as a riding lawnmower.

I bought the stuffed Jingjing on my way to a baseball game. Knowing the International Olympic Committee had sliced America's pastime out of future games, I grabbed the cheapest baseball ticket: Canada versus China.

I forgot that there could be such a thing as a "home team" at the Olympics. Three-quarters of the stadium was yellow-star flags and shrieking. There were only a handful of maple leaves in the ocean of vermillion, inciting my contrarianism, leading me to harken to a faint notion of North American brotherhood.

I planned only to make a mental note of my loyalty. But the game was terribly dull, even for baseball. The Chinese gave up one run and then another. Around the third inning, I decided to experiment. I stood and cupped my hands and screamed, "Get 'em, Canada!" As the game wore on, I yelled more, and my stake in Canada grew. My team kept scoring. I felt flush from the summer air but also from the anticipation of victory.

Could this be, I wondered, the oft-touted life-making passion of sports? The adrenaline shot that keeps us from being the cold, timid creatures Vince Lombardi and before him Teddy Roosevelt had warned us about? I'd begun rooting in boredom, but by inning eight, when the Canadian victory was all but assured, I was swept up in the moment. I fanned my hands, cursed, and stomped on the aluminum bleachers. Meanwhile the rest of the crowd was melting from the loss and the hot August sun. A few of them scooted away.

A little British boy a few benches below turned around and asked, "Mum, what's wrong with that man?"

To which she replied, "He's Canadian, son."

I realized I'd merged my identity with the avatar, become the thing I wasn't. My brain disconnected for a moment, bewildered that the faked passion had led to real sexual-climax-like fervor. Only, and this is the unavoidably depressing thing, the glorious identity was so fleeting. It began to defrost as soon as I left the stadium. By the time I got back to the hostel, my body seemed to have been drained and was ready for another jolt.

This was the blood hook of glory, I think. It must be the urge that pumps through the shoulders of wolves as they close in on a kill, and in the gills of sharks as they filter oxygen-rich ocean and angle toward a leaping seal. Winning is as addictive as any street junk. After digesting, I was empty and needed more.

OVERTIME

When I was growing up, for ten years I went to Red Raider home games, and then when a brain tumor swallowed up my sportswriter father, I stopped. I was visiting him in the hospital one night, and as I left, I saw lights and heard yells and walked over to the stadium nearby to witness a high school baseball match. It was the Broncos versus the Jays, and I wanted to cheer for the Broncos this time, inexplicably, a gut emotion I went with. It turned out the Broncos were the home team, and so this gave me an excuse.

I bought a ticket, two dollars, and some popcorn, two and fifty, and stood by the dugout. As I watched, the Broncos rallied, two runs, then three. A group of boys came over. I wasn't a student, but

I wasn't a parent, So, who was I? they asked. I had rocker hair, so I was cool. I let one of the kids who had fledgling long hair friend me on Facebook. And then the Jays scored a run, and then it was even. A tie was impossible, the Facebook kid told me, as that would mean the Broncos would be out of the championship. The Cowboys would get in.

And it clicked why I wanted the broncs to win. Broncos aren't like jays or bears or bulldogs or wolverines; they are on the verge but not quite humanized. Which is maybe why, feeling self-loathing, I rooted against them at my sushi anniversary dinner. Broncos are in a liminal space between our world and the more-than-human one. Here and out there. Broncos can roam, but saddled up, they become able companions. They are yet unbroken to the rules of humanity in a way I think many of us long to be.

They are an avatar in that we try to give up our souls for the animal and realize that we've been animal all along. As David Abram writes, "Feeling the polyrhythmic pulse of this place—this huge windswept body of water and stone. This vexed being in whose flesh we're entangled." Sometimes I feel becoming mascot is all I can do, flummoxed in a world that so often limits my nature and play to score-charts and costumes.

But is it more natural to pummel and roll in desire? Or to corral and skyscraper? Likely the answer, I think, is the bridge. And so I buck. Up-down, up-down, up-down, up-down. I watch my human self turn animal and then human again, still biting and kicking.

The Broncos won the game, a moment of triumph and pleasure and a fleeting bond established among the fans. There were whistles and song. We basked in the glory, and then left the field in cars to quotidian routines. Some of us slept and snored, our minds slipping into our limbic system, the "animal brain" that lights up in REM sleep.

This is the part of our minds we share with all mammals, which is more activated in sleep than in waking life. Dreaming, we merge.

Water Bugs
A STORY OF ABSOLUTION

Katsaridaphobia is the fear of cockroaches. It is umbrellaed by entomophobia, the panic caused by insects, ten quintillion individuals of which are alive on the earth at any one time.

There are sound reasons to be wary of roaches, as their feces cause asthma in children, and their feet, entomological crampons, carry salmonella and other microbial nemeses that spoil food.

But unlike mosquitoes, our world's deadliest creature, cockroaches do not carry dengue, nor malaria, nor yellow fever, nor West Nile, nor encephalitis. They cannot chew wiring and ignite fires like squirrels. They do not envenomate ankles. They cannot dump their family of four into steel barrels and leave them to decompose in New Hampshire for fifteen years as one human did. And if you're alive, they will not eat you.

There is little that is life threatening, actually, about the scurrying, bark-colored insect—unless you should enter an invertebrate-eating contest as Edward Archbold did. Archbold, a thirty-two-year-old father of two, competed in the bug-munching marathon at a Miami-area reptile store. He sported a ponytail, a yellow tied-dyed T-shirt, and a rocker sweatband. He was required to munch sixty grams of mealworms, thirty-five three-inch-long "super worms," and a bucketful of live giant South American cockroaches, all in hopes of winning an $850 python.

He swallowed many roaches whole. Witnesses say he crammed bugs into his mouth even as the insects crawled out, desperate for light, their antennae twitching at his lips.

Most of the thirty participants bowed out long before the contest's finish. Archbold gorged on the buggy feast and became the "life of the party." He raised his arms in a V, hooting like a football fan. Shortly after winning, Archbold walked out of the store, vomited, and collapsed. An ambulance was phoned for. The paramedics watched Archbold die en route to the hospital.

Doctors examined him and found "airway obstruction by the arthropod body parts." Archbold, the champion devourer of insects, lover of snakes and tie-dye, had been fighting for life even as his last meal had been, too.

There are four thousand species of cockroaches, and most live in rain forests. Only twelve of them are pests. Yet they are, arguably, the world's most abhorred life-form, and I have always wondered why.

In the Dark Ages, citizens brought legal action against roaches. The Bible warns, with its classic redundancy, "Ye shall not make yourselves abominable with any creeping thing that creepeth." The ancient Roman author Pliny the Elder damned them, and early Egyptians conjured spells to ward off roaches.

There are a few theorized causes of ancient entomophobia, the dread that has led to our stomping, poisoning, smashing, damning, wineglass tossing, and eating to death living things that generally do not cause us harm.

Humans, it is thought, frighten at unnatural movement. We watch roaches scurry three miles an hour (at entomological cheetah speeds), and a line of metaphorical ants marches down our nerves.

We humans quiver at prodigious breeding because small individuals, as Napoleon knew, conquer through armies. We also nightmare at creatures smuggling themselves into the cavities of our bodies. Roaches exhibit "positive thigmotaxis," an attraction to squeezes, crawl spaces, cracks, crannies, and drains. Ironically, twentieth-century sanitation allowed roaches to spread throughout homes and other buildings as they followed pipes and cables through spaces in walls and floors. The heat inside our dwellings keeps them alive and breeding in every season.

But I think it is the roaches' otherness that is most damning. They possess the alien look of giant eyes, sprouting antennae, flailing appendages, and wings. They do not voice feelings; their faces do not betray emotion. They are a scurrying mass of unfamiliarity.

Cockroaches are also scavengers, and we detest ragpickers. Think of how vultures, worms, fleas, telemarketers, and the homeless are viewed in our society. They are a reminder of mortality: to see a roach is to envision the day I am aswarm with subterranean recyclers. Seeing a cardboard box's human resident, I remember how possible it is to misplace my life.

Lately I've been thinking of my time in the aptly named Whiteside Elementary School in Lubbock, Texas. I was bullied there, kids flicking my ears and punching me in my then-prodigious belly. Twice I was even stabbed with a pencil. And I've come up with a reason for the discomfort, beyond clichéd preadolescent disquiet. I was not merely a passive victim. I recall gloating over academic accomplishments and gleefully tattling to send troublemakers to the principal's.

I also remember Anna Macon (not her real name), who must have weighed 180 pounds in sixth grade. She had an oval face, freckles, and a 'fro and was, I think now, a melancholic child. Almost daily the boys in my class would swipe her pencils, make fun of her weight, and mock her when she answered questions poorly. I took part in this. We shitheads were shielded by Anna's inability to address our cruelty. Unlike me, Anna never tattled.

Can I be honest and confess how good it felt to be part of the pack? This is a story not often told in the antibullying fervor of schools today. Everyone wants to be a victim, or to protect one. I was stabbed with a pencil, but I also cherished Anna because she provided a buffer. Who doesn't enjoy, at least in secret, the sensation and opportunity of squishing a life beneath you? And the trick, they say, when the wolves are out, is to run faster than the person who is closest to you.

———

Googling "roaches" one day, I discovered article after article about how police regard the presence of bugs as reason to take people's children away.

One mother of five in Roswell, Georgia, wasn't around to receive a knock from the police when the neighbors called about her kids, claiming they were running wild in the neighborhood. Police found roaches covering the walls and some falling from the ceiling. The kids were removed into protective custody.

A baby was found being eaten by roaches in Oklahoma in 2015. The infant had died from SIDS, not insects. SIDS is the leading cause of infant death in America. Roaches will eat dead things. Still, police arrested the mother and put her other children in protective custody.

In February 2013 in Beverly Hills, Florida, teachers discovered a roach in a nine-year-old's ear. His parents were arrested, and the boy was placed in alternative care.

Police find roaches to be indicative of larger issues, but in Miami, 32 percent of houses report roach infestation. In Houston it's 38 percent, Atlanta 25, New Orleans 41.

My friend George Getschow is a hard-wrought, twinkle-eyed cowboy journalist, a luminary in the literary nonfiction world. He lives on the shores of a humming lake in Texas. One night he woke to what felt like a wild animal burrowing in his ear. As he screamed, his wife grabbed a flashlight and caught a glimpse of an alien slithering into his skull. At this moment, George's cries convinced his teenage daughter that he was being murdered, and she hid in a closet.

At the hospital George threatened to punch out a physician. He had to be drugged and held down by four people as the doctor tonged out from George's head a cockroach the size of his thumb. The doc said it was not uncommon for roaches to find their way into homes, into people. Maybe four or five times a week, the hospital saw patients running through the doors screaming, near suicide, with bugs in their ears.

———

Once, a few years ago, I woke in the night to what I thought was a raindrop on my bare inner thigh. Then I remembered that I was indoors; the faux droplet was a wet roach that had landed near one of my body's cavities. I knew because I'd seen roaches rain from the air-conditioning vent in the living room. I called my landlord's exterminator and described the intruder: an inch long, jet black, alien looking.

"They're just water bugs," the exterminator said in a gruff Texan drawl. "Hard to kill."

"They're not roaches?"

"Naw, they're water bugs; they live here. They got lost going up your house."

It was novel to me then, quaint even, to imagine a poor, confused roachlike-but-not-roach creature ascending my two-story apartment, a wayward forest traveler entering my home, thinking I lived in a tree. Water bugs carried no association of salmonella, asthma, or George's ear.

But the exterminator, like roach feet, was full of shit. Water bugs are a species called oriental cockroaches, ironically from Africa, and live near humans, indoors and out. They can't live, now, anywhere else. After thousands of years, this species has evolved to require human habitation.

Like it, my ancestors, some of the first white Europeans in America, are said to have "discovered," "settled," "made," and "colonized" America, instead of having invaded it. We have stayed so long, many consider us the "original" population.

Cockroaches were a part of those early settlements. After returning from Jamestown, Englishman John Smith moaned about another invader in America's first white settlement. In 1624 he wrote, "A certaine India Bug, called by the Spaniards a Cacarootch, the which creeping into Chests they eat and defile with their ill-scented dung." This is perhaps the first record of roaches in America.

From a historical standpoint, there is justification for neither white people nor roaches to be living here. We are colonists still, like Smith and that early roach. And like many invader children, I've been brought from somewhere, a point of origin from which my kind radiated. But I don't know how, after generations of evolution, to live anywhere else.

The word "roach" came into use when Europeans began casting their seed and spreading their progeny across the world. First Europeans imported the insects from Africa, and then they exported them to new continents. Now the word has taken on meaning as an metaphorical slight. Around the world, in disparate cultures, to call someone a "cacarootch" is an unambiguous insult.

Thus the Tutsis were cockroaches in 1994. Criminals in New York City, according to police commissioner Howard Safir in 1996, were cockroaches. In 2002 Rush Limbaugh berated Mexicans for breeding like cockroaches. In 2015, according to UK columnist Katie Hopkins, African migrants invaded Europe like cockroaches.

Every hierarchy has its lowest caste—and its outcasts. Lower classes know they are within a system. The outsiders provide a buffer, a reassurance that one is not a pariah. But take out hierarchy, and not only does this liberate the bottom rungs, it shakes the foundations from the lives of everyone else up top. Every creature comes raining down.

Carl Jung believed our basic drives were insectlike. "The unconscious was an insect" for Jung, says Charlotte Sleigh. He also thought a dream of roaches was simply the unconscious communicator lodging a complaint against the dreamer.

Franz Kafka's Gregor Samsa taps into the archetypal fear when, with his form morphed into a human-sized bug, he terrifies his family. They secrete him, hiding him from the light until slowly, alienated, he wastes away.

In "On the Pleasure of Hating" William Hazlitt wrote, "Nature seems (the more we look into it) made up of antipathies: without something to hate, we should lose the very spring of thought and action."

I needed Anna Macon. For without her, I was her.

———

For two decades a man in Plano, Texas, operated the Cockroach Hall of Fame as part of his extermination business. Michael Bohdan, the owner of the Cockroach Hall of Fame, is a silver-haired, stout, square-headed man who people call Cockroach Dundee. His signature attire: a fedora studded with taxidermied cockroaches.

He said in an interview, "Cockroaches have been around for 350 million years, and my feeling is, is that for any insect that can get by the onslaught of stuff that's been thrown at them, maybe we can learn from them."

Bohdan exhibited dead cockroaches reclining on bath towels and in beach chairs, cockroaches in place of the Statue of Liberty's flame, cockroaches dressed as Elvis in his fat, jumpsuit period. Dressed as Marilyn Monroach, David Letteroach, Ross Peroach, Imelda Marcoroach (in an emerald dress with gold shoes). And there was a roach version of the Bates Motel, complete with a tiny dead roach mother waiting on the porch.

One roach was decked out in a white fur cape, seated behind a minipiano and candelabra, flimsy roach forelegs on tiny piano keys, with a sign that read NOW APPEARING: LIBEROACHI.

And, of course, as you might have guessed, there was a Last Supper with roaches, presided over by a cockroach Jesus.

Can a cockroach Jesus offer absolution?

Many Americans don't know, or forget as I did, that our national bird, our bald eagle—a graceful fighter jet with wings—subsists on carrion, along with its fish. That up to three pounds of scavenging bacteria reside in our intestines and keep us alive. That our eukaryotic cells, which make us look human, formed millions of years ago as mutual cooperation among different invading bacteria and archaea. That when trash collectors cease working, garbage heaps up, as it did during the New York City sanitation strike of 1968.

Fossils of cockroaches go back 325 million years. That means they are 150 million years older than dinosaurs, 324,800,000 years older than humans. Every other insect found in the geologic layer of the first roaches has gone extinct. Sometimes the period when the oldest roaches are found, the Carboniferous, is called the Age of Cockroaches. Timeless scavengers make up the rock upon which we stand.

Biologists who study cats have lately supported a new theory of domestication. Rather than humans choosing pets, our four-legged companions are parasites who gradually ingratiated themselves with us so that they might survive. These encounters remind me that there will never be an isolated phenomenon known as "humanity." With even our guts swimming in civilizations, with mitochondria and house cats becoming part of our lives, maybe one day roaches, too, will become indispensable. The once invaders our companions.

"We have never been one, we have never been individuals," says posthumanist theorist Donna Haraway. "We're compost."

One day at school, I saw Anna's father, a mild-mannered man with a barrel chest and spectacles. He was dressed in jeans and a white T-shirt and seemed conscientious toward Anna and our teacher. It was clear Anna looked up to him with reverence.

Another day, during the school's talent show, Anna karaoked "Pretty Woman," which she said was her dad's favorite. I hadn't the courage to sing, to juggle, to back flip. I was too terrified of stares, of what would be said when I could hear and when I couldn't. I was afraid, I think, of the things I said to Anna, afraid that the nefarious bully I projected, which was what I was capable of, was me.

I imagine I made fun of Anna's singing later. But inside, in a way I couldn't have articulated, I was awed that she, who was always so quiet, so stomped on, had the gumption to bellow a song to her idol, to declare her love, to reach out and strike back at all those dipshits who had tried so hard to step on her.

For about a month while his ear healed, George and his family slept with earplugs. They sprayed pesticides weekly. Then, as the paranoia wore off, they put away their plugs and their poison.

Once, a roach entomologist in Gainesville, Florida, helped a woman overcome her lifelong katsaridaphobia. Everywhere she went, she was pursued by roaches, and she couldn't stop thinking about them. They colored her every day with fearful possibility. Were they in the cereal? Under the park bench? In the bag of dog food? The entomologist was not trained in psychology, but he put her on a regimen of exposure therapy. They started small by talking. Then they progressed to photographs. Then an examination of dead, pinned roaches. Then live ones behind glass. After several visits, her hyperventilating ceased. Her nightmares evaporated. The culmination of the therapy was the day she held a live roach in her gloved hand. They stared at each other, one creature to another, over the distance of her arm, antennae twitching. It had come to this: she and the roach were limb in limb.

A Passage of Birds

My nephew and I were on the patio of my sister's farmhouse when a thunk pulled us from our storybook. A common female house sparrow had soared into a window. Its legs looked shattered, wings mangled, a blow to the skull against a pane of glass as wide as a tractor. The bird had, as some thirty million a year do, mistaken transparency for passage.

The house sparrow, along with the starling and rock pigeon, is one of the most common birds in North America. It was once an exotic imported to Brooklyn from Europe but is now as regular as taxes.

The bird was dying, as my nephew Oliver could plainly see, and in the way of five-year-olds it became The Most Important Thing. His cherubic cheeks, question-mark mouth, glistening blue eyes reflected unforgiveness. *Was I going to let the little bird die?*

This was hardly his first brush with death. Oliver's guinea pigs had died the year before. As had his hamsters. Not to mention the chickens my sister and her husband kept that fell prey to weasels, coyotes, stray dogs, hawks, and, that year, the Texas heat.

Not to mention his grandfather, a man whom Oliver remembered only as the writhing, pale geriatric who couldn't walk. The man who ballooned to 250 pounds and shrank to 180 depending on his medications. Grandpa who sounded like a diesel engine and who couldn't remember his name. But he called Oliver sweet pea or sweetie-petey-pie or half a dozen other endearments that were good enough.

Oliver remembered Grandpa's wheezing breath (like stale biscuits), the constant wheelchair and chapped skin (like tissue paper), the penetrating expression, the parted gray hairdo (Grandpa's last vanity), and the nostril hairs that grew into hog bristle candy canes.

Oliver, though, will never know the motorcycle racer who chickened aboard Kawasakis, helmetless. The sports journalist who mysteriously seemed to meet friends wherever he went until it became annoying for anybody traveling with him. Who remembered to tell his kids his affections when he picked them up from school.

Oliver will never know the man who did cocaine and drank heavily and stared through the windshield as if he could cut a way to a better life. Who could be the angry Homer Simpson strangulating his son, which in real life hurt like a noose.

Oliver will miss both ends of the spectrum, the admirable and cocky and insecure and sullen. Oliver will only carry in his memory this soft, vulnerable old man, just as he could only cradle this sparrow after it meteored into a window, missing the wide open plain just beyond the home.

I could see the inevitable, and so could Oliver, I think. Only, my nephew was still in the Snow White world that is etched into us Americans—a journalist changing in a phone booth, a lifesaving measure, a secret pill, a Disney ending.

Now, could I supply him one?

Two parts drove me: to shield and to teach. To comfort and to let Oliver know, as I fear so many do not, that death is as much part of what we're set down with as the wings that let us soar over our troubles when we may. I usually don't have time to ask these kinds of questions at the moment, but my senses were sharpened because I believed Oliver might connect the bird to his grandfather who had just died two months before. I thought it might help him understand something about his leaving.

So what was there to do? The bird had a broken leg, to be sure, probably two. The sparrow bobbed on its side like a cork and blinked and seemed alertly alive. Its wings stretched, and then suddenly it flew away for a tear-jerkingly happy half-second. But it nosedived through a rosebush and landed in fallen petals. A final touchdown, it seemed. The bird flopped over, eyes blinking in the sun.

Oliver wailed for me to do something.

Grandpa's death was not easy, eleven years after the brain surgery that emasculated him when I was eighteen. Overnight he became an elderly man. Old *woman* is what I thought when the ICU nurses showed me to his bed. I remember thinking there must have been a mix-up, some deleted paperwork. I peeled back the veil-thin curtain and saw the shriveled pea body rolled into the fetal position at the top corner of his mattress. His thumbs were pressed against his lips. Not the weightlifter who should have filled the bed.

Many pills later, a divorce from my mother, his four strokes and ministrokes—a slow melt and steady march to blackout as life took away his abilities and the clarity to remember the names of his family.

Many people watch their fathers and grandmothers and wives and husbands and children and friends dying; they witness the same fluttering, same diving conclusion as minds lose altitude. What's remarkable, I think, is that as a society we're becoming more public about dying, willing to watch others take the plunge. You can witness almost any kind of death on the Internet. You can google countless caught-in-their-last-acts of people in scenarios as complicated as skydiving stunt doubles careening off each other, or as quotidian as a retiree snoring as his ventilator is switched off.

In 1936 when Robert Capa snapped his "Falling Soldier" photo of a man shot in the Spanish Civil War, it was controversial (before it was revealed fake) because a person was dying *before our eyes*. When men came back from war, they were expected not to talk, to get on with their lives and maintain equanimity. Vulnerability, the allowance that something had shattered them, was unacceptable. "Therapy" wasn't a term fixed in our vocabulary, though "toughness" was.

We've made progress in the twenty-first century. We accept that people have counselors, Wounded Warrior Projects, terms for the terrors and horrors of bloody death, and ways to heal. We have support groups and rights watches. This isn't to say we can't go much further, but what I want to ask here is: how does a young boy hold in his mind the two disparate thoughts, that masculinity is toughness as still taught by media and society, and, a lesson learned by necessity, that to be human means frailty?

So I searched and searched, while we held the dying bird, for an answer to how much I should impart to my nephew—the monkey brain inside me looking for patterns and clues the way my dad's roommates searched for the zillionth piece on the desk-sized *Titanic* puzzle. I wanted to say to Oliver that Grandpa learned humility in the end, accepting his place and that there was nothing unmanly about being cared for in old age. But the former wouldn't be true as the latter surely is.

It was impossible for my father to accept his condition, partly because he was thrust into it at the relatively young age of fifty-nine. His abilities didn't slowly wink out; he was cut off. He had been a constant traveler, always on a plane or bus with some sports team, and now at the end of his life he was house arrested by his body. He took this frustration out on my mother, as many do, until it drove her away.

Oliver picked up the bird to inspect.

"A cast for its wing," he suggested.

"How about a Tupperware container?" I asked. Something he could do and let me think. While he was gone, I thought to the bird, *Now what would you like us to do?* The bird blinked.

My mind felt directed to the woods at the edge of the property, a still-wild copse of magnolias, maples, and mesquites, harborer of animals and abundant avian life. A good place for a passage into the after-bird-world. My nephew returned with the plastic tub, and we placed the wounded inside. I felt the heartbeat, which was slower than I expected but still chirruping. The bird bobbled its head, tried to flap and crawl over the lip of the bowl.

"No!" Oliver cried. "We can't let it escape. It might die."

"Oliver," I said. "Sometimes it's things' time. They pass on."

"No!" he cried, and let the tears glide. "It can't."

Visiting my father, commuting from college and grad school to his last nursing home, I had gotten close to my sister who cared for Dad, close to my little nephew—this new boy, fresh faced, raised on chickens as much as plasma TVs, steadily edging into the street world of adults. Oliver, I knew, looked up to me as an intermediary. Not like his father, who was perhaps too "authority," and not like his grandfather, but a man who had no other adults left to look up to. A liminal figure.

There was a consciousness I had that, yes, lying in that Tupperware, no matter what story I tried to cobble, was pure unadulterated chance. The bird could have flown wide, missed the bright window. Just as it wasn't in my dad's power to control the amorphous tentacle of undetectable cancer.

A mark of insecurity, I'm told by one social scientist, is the need to control. Resigning power is often seen as weak in society, but inevitably we hit the plateau of our ability. I've come to believe that there can be a choice, a powerful turn down the river to see things in story, to see reasons and purpose and how we can learn. My dad needed humility. And this bird needed, maybe, to teach this child and teach me too about dying.

But maybe there was no purpose here, because that thought too strikes me now as my mind trying to lasso death into an understanding. Just like Oliver, perhaps I was unaware of how I was trying to bring back from the brink something that could only slip over.

"Yes, Oliver," I said, not sure I was on the right path. "That's just nature. Birds die too. It's okay for them to die."

"No! No!" He fist-balled the tears until they coated his cheeks like morning dew.

His mother came out and rubbed his halo of blond hair. "Oh, Oliver," she said.

Following a moment of his tears, I said, "Oliver, we need to take the bird over to the woods. We're probably going to give it a heart attack if we leave it here and keep manhandling it."

"What's manhandle?" he said.

"When you mess with things too much," his mother said.

"Look," I said, eventually, "the bird started to fly there." I pointed to the copse. "I think that's where we should take it; it's where it wants to be. That's where it was headed."

So we did, walking across the three acres with the chickens and goats at our ankles to the trees and barb wire. Oliver set the bird in the brush, and it scrambled out from the tub and under the wire. The bird keeled over on its side, body lifting ever so imperceptibly with its heart.

"We'll come back tonight," Oliver demanded. "If it's still here, we take it back inside, okay?"

"Okay."

For a distraction on the way back, I mentioned all the life that surrounded us, the visible worms and squirrels and crows and blue jays and cicadas and goats and all my sister's fat hens that pecked through the lawn and made their slow way to a corn dinner.

I returned to the woods later that night. The boy had forgotten, but you never know. Sometimes a child's memory picks up cleanly where it leaves off in a way adults can only envy.

The broken sparrow was in the same spot, staring up at the dark sky. The ground around us hushed. An opening appeared in the barbed wire. Someone or something had manipulated an entrance just big enough for me (another piece or another puzzle?), and I bent down and squeezed through, sliding against the scratchy leaves. The bird flapped and limped away through some tricky thorns until it was cradled in a hollow at the base of a maple tree. *Ants will get it if I don't,* I thought. But when I touched the encasing vines, I realized they were nettles, and my fingers came up stinging.

Anger welled up, directed at the bird. And I stepped back, realizing it must be like the rage, though milder, that my father had felt, directed at my mother. The same feeling I'd had at Thanksgiving two years earlier when Dad was very fat and tired, eyes rolling into the back of his head, when he'd wet himself at my sister's house.

I wheeled him to the bathroom and balanced him while I peeled off the sweatpants and boxers. My brother-in-law's unassuming, toupeed father, Jerry, came in, and when I tried to tell him there was no problem, Jerry said that he had been an army medic in Korea and had seen it all.

"A little piss in your pants is nothing to what I've seen, Clint. I've held guts in my hands," he said, and I rolled off my dad's underwear.

"Innards," he repeated.

Somehow this helped, and Jerry offered some boxer-briefs and this did too. But the only extra pants around were too small, and changing my standing, overweight father was like assisting the birth of a calf while balancing two sacks of rice on my shoulders. Dad told me his knees were buckling, and I realized he had feces smeared on his ass.

I covered and cleaned him, and Jerry offered again to help. I refused at first, illogically afraid and ashamed. But Jerry persisted.

"I've picked up limbs from the dust, man!"

I relented, smiling at Jerry's audacity. Jerry balanced my father while I cleaned him, a relatively ordinary task if I thought about it—what I do to myself every day.

Pants and underwear changed, I listened to more of Jerry's war stories. He said that a man's balls were an inconvenient organ, like the tonsils. "Always in the way," he said. At the sick bays where Jerry had worked, newbie medics were afraid to touch testicles until they had to get to a leg or a part of the stomach. Then they soon got over it.

While I changed my father, this was the first time I'd thought of testicles as inconvenient, as disposable. At eighteen I'd simply gotten furious at my father's emasculation and had maintained the trickle of ferocity for years. When I saw my father curled up like an aging matriarch for the first time, I had cared principally not because of what happened to him but what was happening to me.

At my sister's house on Thanksgiving, watching my father wash his milky hands in a marble basin, I saw the delicacy in his stuttered movements, the certainty in his curled lips, and the grandeur of his receding hair. I knew I had a father, someone to compare myself to and grow against—a vine curling around an aging trunk. I knew my father was going to die, and he would die slowly, completely, and show me the way in front, even if he did it imperfectly. My father, for his ills, was still my model for how to go out of this world. As I would be, to whoever came next—if not my own child, then maybe, at least in part, to Oliver.

I had come back to the woods hoping the bird would be gone. But this, I realized, was like hoping for death not to exist—that for me, for Oliver, everyone, we'd get a pass, on the wheelchair, on cancer, on life's end. On big windows that seem clear but are as impossible to break through as life's riddles. In the dark, while my anger chilled, the bird flapped its wings a little and watched. I know I was projecting, but the bird seemed as gracious about all this as my dad in his best moments, unruffled about what had to happen, about the cold night to come.

Oliver remembered later and asked me if the bird was still there. I lied then and said that when I'd checked, the sparrow had been gone. I woke early the next morning and went out to the maple tree to see if the bird was there and to move him if so. As I walked along the wet grass, the fog lifted from the prairie, the roosters crowed, and somewhere eggs hatched. I saw that my lie and my hope from the day before had become true.

The Color of Tarsiers

We are walking through a forest where rain falls on the broad acacia leaves, pooling near the mud and roots that catch our ankles.
The air snatches at my neck. I come over a hill, not too far from
the front desk that has maps of ranges and messages on the walls
that begin with help: "Help the Tarsiers," "Help the environment,"
"Help the Philippines."

The man who was speaking on our bus told us the park is free,
but we should buy something if we feel we should.

"The people who work here make no money," he said. He was
staring out the window when he mentioned this, as markets and
mangroves passed by.

When I see the first tarsier, it is asleep on a branch, its mouse
tail twisted around the stem of a leaf, rumpled fur wet in the down-
pour. I have to hurry after a cursory glance, because there is a bigger
group behind ours, urging us on, disappointment already in their
faces and footsteps.

I follow our guide, winding around a corkscrew path and in
pockets of pea green leaves the size of quarters. The second tarsier
is shaded and dry. The primate opens its eyes, swivels its head 190
degrees. They are nocturnal, but a dozen of us are taking pictures
and crunching leaves. We're loudly making plans for drinking and
the conference back at the hotel.

We march to the third tarsier, high up in a palm tree. Our young
guide, a man with brutal side chops and a Chicago Cubs cap, points
with a piece of bamboo.

"You see," he says. "They like high ground."

It looks comforting to be up there in the shade of the palm from rain and sun, and just out of earshot of our cameras. Our shutters click like eyelids fluttering. This tarsier doesn't wake.

Somehow it hits us all at once: the lack of sleep from travel, the jet lag, the hunger for lunch. We are on a vacation, yet we move heads down, feet shuffling as if we're bearing a load.

We hear from our guide that there are only ten tarsiers in this park, and only about two hundred in the wild around this island where they are indigenous. They are small, narrow boned, easy to break. Visitors sometimes want the apple-sized primates as pets, but holding one could shatter it.

"You may think the tarsiers are cute," the guide says, "but they are not your babies."

Elsewhere on the island there are what the guide calls "concentration camps," laboratories where tarsiers are kept in pens and taken out, put on people's shoulders. Each tarsier lasts about a year there, he says, in that sparkling pet shop, and so new ones are taken from the wild to fill the cages.

At our fourth and last view, I bend down and my face gets as close to a tarsier as it will be to my own hand later when I take out my wallet and hold it up to count the bills. I see the tarsier folded into a shape like a fist, his wet fur smooth, fleshy, his owl head buried into his chest. He is breathing—a slight ripple of peach fuzz undulating up and down, about one breath per long second. His ears branch off into a Y, and his tail hangs down thin and brittle like a stalactite.

A little quake echoes in my stomach. A sleeping heart, I think. A pumping fist (it's about the size of my heart), beating, breathing, sending blood through the forest and the island.

I come into the gift store, where there is a spotted dog walking around hungry and a glass case selling watches, key chains, sunglasses, small bags, T-shirts, and postcards of wide-eyed tarsiers.

After we pay for what we want, we drive away down a tree-lined dirt road, my arm on the window sill, as another bus passes us on the way in. And though I believe I should feel red, all I can think about, all I can see out the window, is green.

The Carp Experience

On a cloudy day in December, the Chicago Canal Dam spans what looks like any other polluted stream of gray water. At a cost of nine million dollars in construction and five hundred thousand dollars every year in operations, the dam isn't visible. It lurks, like what it's meant to keep out, below the surface. A barge should and does pass through every hour.

The dam is an electric current that runs across the canal, charging 1,500 feet of water between mile markers 296.1 and 296.7. Two volts pass throughout the water, enough to kill a child or an elderly person or someone with a bad heart and enough to impair the unborn infant of a pregnant mother. It sends sparks flying from the hulls of barges. Everyone, from fishers to dock workers, is advised not to touch any surface in contact with the water.

Its enemies, Asian carp, have no stomachs. They can weigh up to one hundred pounds and eat 40 percent of their body weight each day. They are vacuums, hoovering up whatever they can from the cold water, usually phytoplankton and zooplankton, microscopic bottom feeders that form the base of a river's food pyramid. Carp cut out the middlemen and everything else at the top because nothing, apart from not-so-picky human anglers, can eat the carp.

Carp also eat the eggs of other fish, infanticide being an impressively good takeover strategy. The carp in turn lay five million eggs a season.

These carp are threatening to cross into the Great Lakes and decimate $7 billion worth of American fisheries.

The fish at the gates of the Great Lakes are really five subspecies lumped together and called Asian for shorthand. The silver carp is perhaps the most famous. It is known as the "jumping fish" or "flying fish" and is easily seen on YouTube in its most famous habit, when scared by motorboats, of leaping en masse up to ten feet in the air. The fish slap boaters in the face. They can break noses and jaws. They have knocked people unconscious. Wildlife personnel wear face masks when attempting to catch them.

In 2009 the attorney general of Michigan filed a lawsuit against the State of Illinois to close the canal. In January of 2010, the Supreme Court heard the case but denied the request. In July of the same year, Michigan filed again, this time with Minnesota, Ohio, Pennsylvania, and Wisconsin, in a joint lawsuit against the Army Corps of Engineers to shut the canal and stop the fish.

There was no other reason for these actions, state against state and states against the nation, except the prevention of the bottom-feeding creature from spoiling the Great Lakes catch.

I want to pay attention to the carp, this chubby, suctioning plague fish that caused states to sue, fishers to panic, the Army Corps of Engineers to build its dam and later dump gallons of poison, because I'm about to suggest that, maybe, we haven't been as generous as we should about this species in a place where it hasn't been before.

 But I want to think about Molly first, the Hypophthalmichthys molitrix. Molly is an average silver carp, who weighs thirty pounds and is the color of a U.S. quarter. She swims in schools of about a hundred, each of whom can release pheromones to attract fellow silvers. Molly prefers low-velocity, high-volume streams, taller than a person.

When Molly was born, she was a pinhead-sized embryo in an egg that was waterlogged. Her mother laid her and a partial clutch during the warm flood season. Carp must lay eggs in rivers swift and long enough to carry their kin from larva to youth. They are born in transit. Molly floated in mid-current for about a hundred hours before hatching.

Her defining moments are birth, death, motherhood, and swimming into new territory. Like most creatures when an area is overcrowded, Molly will relocate, a slow glide into waters more habitable, where there are nutrients, rivers less teeming with sizable, leaping cousins.

CHINA

Molly's ancestors came up the Mississippi from the South. One theory is that the Asian carp were originally brought to Arkansas in the 1970s from China to clean sewage-plant tanks, hog-swill lagoons, and other detritus-filled lakes. But one summer, heavy rains raised the Arkansas ponds until water and carp spilled into neighboring streams, which led them to the Chicago River.

Recent evidence partially undermines this theory. Accounts of free carp are reported from Louisiana before those of Arkansas. In Louisiana they may have been humanely released, dumped when assumed dead, or deliberately introduced for sport as so many other fish are.

Either way, Molly now lives in America's largest river, while her brethren occupy the waters of twelve states and Puerto Rico. To mate, find food, and make a family, Molly must move. And thus carp are nuzzling the Chicago Shipping Canal's electric door, so many miles from the ponds where they were supposed to clean up or get caught on a hook.

Michigan writer Joe Abramajtys equates the Asian carp's plight to the "schizophrenic" American immigrant experience: "They are brought in to do the shit work other, older, established groups shun—forced to live in camps and ghettos . . . discriminated and legislated against . . . until some of them escape their plight to live free in better circumstances." If Molly were to get shocked in the Chicago Canal, the two volts twisting through her body, there is a chance it wouldn't kill her. Stunned, Molly could regain consciousness on the other side of the dam. There is a notion that, perhaps, a carp like her already has.

It is human ingenuity and, fittingly, immigrant exploitation that has allowed the carp this far upstream. Completed in the year 1900, the canal reversed the direction of the water to create the only river in the world to flow away from its mouth. The American Public Works Association (APWA) labeled it "one of the top ten public works projects of the century." The American Society of Civil Engineers has said it is one of the Seven Wonders of the Modern World. And it is registered as a historic landmark.

The canal's primary function is to divert human sewage.

Up until the twentieth century, Chicagoans dumped their waste into Lake Michigan, from which they also piped drinking water. In 1885, flooding backed up over the potable intakes. Ninety thousand people died from typhoid, dysentery, and cholera: 450 times more than died in the Great Chicago Fire.

The canal was the country's largest municipal earth-moving project and the largest human-made canal ever completed at the time. According to the APWA, the construction was a key event for the building of the Panama Canal because the Chicago Canal trained its engineers.

The Chicago Canal was begun in 1892 and finished eight back-breaking years later. It required 41 million cubic yards of rock and soil displacement. The 85,000 workers were immigrants from Ireland, Poland, and other Eastern European countries, as well as many African Americans. They were made to do the hardest and dirtiest work. They dug by actual hand, as in the early twentieth century power tools and steam shovels were in their infancy. These newcomers, freshly welcomed to American urban life from many parts of the globe, removed a quantity of earth and glacier debris that would equal a square mile of buildings each five stories tall.

The Chicago Shipping and Sanitary Canal became not just an architectural and engineering marvel but a concentrated piece of public reconciliation, progress that was Chicago's upward trajectory following a municipal self-poisoning and the perhaps mythic lamp-kicking, barn-burning cow. And it was done on the backs of immigrants.

Their work reversed many millennia of gravity. Today the Chicago River flows *away* from Lake Michigan. The canal sends water and waste into the Mississippi, which continues down to the bayou where it dumps pesticides from Iowa, mercury from the factories in Ohio, and Chicago citizens' morning flushes.

Then as now, a neighboring state sued to close the Chicago Canal. The attorney general of Missouri claimed that discharging metropolitan manure in the Mississippi might send the waste into St. Louis's drinking glasses. And, then as now, there was concern in the other Great Lakes states, in that instance concern that the six hundred thousand cubic feet of water flowing out of Lake Michigan every minute would empty the lake like a balloon deflating from a puncture. But Missouri failed in its lawsuit, as the five states later would, and the passage to the lakes, dug by immigrants, was left open.

Carp weren't the first aquatic arrivals. Tanker ships have brought a formidable array of international visitors: 183 documented exotics in the Great Lakes, including zebra mussels, quagga mussels, flatworms, humpback pea clams, European flounder, spiny water fleas, an Ebola-ish fish-killing virus, and the famous sea lamprey. Lamprey are eel-like creatures with circular rows of sharp teeth and piercing tongues that clamp onto the bodies of fish and suck out their bodily fluids.

Zebra mussels have spread to every tributary of the Mississippi south of Minnesota, and there are now more than one trillion quagga mussels in the Great Lakes.

And, of course, there are the Pacific salmon. These fish that the attorney general of Michigan is so worried about need to be stocked each year. The salmon are stunned by electricity in their home rivers out west and snatched as eggs from their mothers. They are not native, as neither is the rainbow trout or the brown trout, the latter a fish that is now artificially stocked in more than five hundred rivers in the United States.

And you probably shouldn't eat the Great Lakes salmon anyway, because of all the petrochemicals, pesticides, and heavy metals pouring in from the Rust Belt, especially if you're young or elderly or pregnant. That is, the same people who shouldn't swim in the Chicago Shipping Canal.

Zebra mussels, though, while devastating to some natives, have improved water quality. Each mussel can filter a liter of water per day. Filtering contaminants, in turn, has increased the populations of invertebrates (ironically the backbone of aqua systems) and yellow perch, and the mussels have also helped recover native walleyes, lake trout, and emerald shiners.

Asian carp can be remarkably healthy eating. They are low in mercury, because they don't eat other fish, and high in cancer-fighting Omega-3s. The carp are bony, which leads Americans to view them with suspicion, but the Chinese eat them all the time. Another irony: in China carp are sometimes overfished.

And this is the point where I begin to question the validity of warnings against invasives. The red flags seem part of a neo-nationalist impulse, the flagrant isolationism that kept immigrants in social dry dock as they built our cities. I'm not suggesting we open all our wildernesses to invaders, but I want to consider how immigrant species might become stitched into the fabric of our national ecosystem, as it seems pretty obvious we're not going to get rid of them.

Louisiana chef Philippe Parola, a French immigrant, was trolling the Atchafalaya River for a unique fish to cook on the legendary Jeff Corwin's Extreme Cuisine show. Parola thought he could find alligator gar to impress Corwin, but he changed his mind when two giant carp jumped above his boat and landed right at his feet. Since then he has written a book on the fish, hosted cooking demonstrations, held community cooking classes, and posts recipes on the Internet that all use Asian carp. He has licensed the moniker "silverfin" for the carp in hopes that a new name, a strategy of many immigrants, will help its reception.

Parola calls the meat "as white as snow" and has said that "there is no better fish" and he would "take it over tilapia." He has pioneered invasive species culinary arts. "Can't beat 'em, eat 'em!" he says.

Silverfin Provencale needs, along with four silverfin steaks, four tablespoons of olive oil, four ounces of white wine, lemon juice, fresh garlic, onion, one diced tomato, parsley, and seasoning to taste and should be baked and served over pasta or mashed potatoes.

Former Illinois governor Pat Quinn said publicly while still in office that he was a fan of the Asian carp. And Feeding Illinois, an anti-hunger advocacy group, is excited about using the carp to feed the 1.8 million people who rely on Illinois's Supplemental Nutrition Program. They have held cooking demonstrations with Chef Parola at local high schools.

Perhaps in time Americans will begin to see the carp as desirable. Perhaps silverfin will become a celebrated comfort food like fried chicken. Perhaps anglers will cast their hooks hoping not for a trout but for an edible, healthy alternative. Then wildlife personnel won't have to ship in eggs every season and stun mother salmon. Maybe we will embrace the once-foreign carp as quintessentially American like many things, including "America."

Despite the barrier's construction in 2006, evidence of the carp above the electric current has been found numerous times in DNA sampling. One theory put forward by the Illinois Department of Natural Resources is that people in Chicago's Chinatown along the Chicago River are releasing the fish into the water. Immigrant Chinese, the DNR claims, will buy carp and set them free as a karmic gesture atoning for the sin of eating flesh. But it was a Caucasian American, a trucker, who was busted in 2012 by undercover agents in Michigan for driving around and selling live carp out of his flatbed.

Should the carp swim en masse above the barrier, past the electricity and lawsuits, there is little authorities could do to reverse that flow. But the dangers of the carp are possibly overstated. They may not like the cold North, and they may not be adapted to the larger lakes' surface. They require the smooth, narrow, moving channels of living water. Or they could evolve to live like other stocked fish, stolen from their homelands and thrust into harsh habitats across the country.

———

During a routine maintenance closure, the Department of Natural Resources and the Army Corps of Engineers teamed up with some three hundred other organizations to dump 2,200 gallons of rotenone poison into the Chicago Shipping Canal, targeting the Asian carp. Rotenone, according to its Material Safety Data Sheet, is toxic and carcinogenic, targets the liver, kidneys, nerves, and female reproductive system, and could harm an unborn child. It should be handled with a "self-contained breathing apparatus." Its "chemical, physical, and toxicological properties have not been thoroughly investigated."

Officials poured the poison from jugs into a six-mile stretch of the Chicago Shipping Canal. Two hundred thousand pounds of native fish rose to the water's surface: red, white, and blue and asphyxiated. A single silverfin floated with them.

Recycle Prairie Dogs

In the driveway of a farmhouse outside Lubbock, Texas, Lynda Watson, age sixty-four, greets me wearing a grimace-smile, short gray hair, and a dust-covered banana-slug-yellow T-shirt that reads "Recycle Prairie Dogs."

"Filthy creatures," she says, cocking her head. She refers not to the rodents in her shed but to the college-age men who rent her house, now awash in garbage. "I never go in there."

Instead of visiting her paying human tenants, Lynda will choose to wilt for ten hours in the Texas July sun, sticking her hands into darkened burrows and retrieving rodents who reward her by trying to tear her fingers off.

The *Houston Chronicle* once called Lynda Watson "A random fragment in the social order." She claims to have rescued about two thousand prairie dogs a year for the last thirty years, which would be more than any other person in the world.

In response to a phoned request to tag along on her prairie dog rescuing, she said, "As long as you can shut up and pay attention, we'll get along. Because the minute I put my hand on an animal, I'm responsible for him. The mission is him and not spreading your words. Honest to god, I don't give a rat's ass about your story."

Prairie dogs hail from the squirrel family, five species all told, burrowing from Mexico to Saskatchewan. Their homes resemble a dirt version of a McDonald's playground: tunneled matrices that descend ten feet and stretch for up to thirty, spaces inside for bedrooms, bathrooms, a foyer, and nurseries for the bald, blind new-borns.

For their pains digging mansions, prairie dogs get invaded by rattlesnakes and black-footed ferrets, who depend on rodent meat. In total, up to eighty-nine species rely on prairie dogs or their burrows. For this, scientists dub them a "keystone species."

Which makes it perplexing how much prairie dogs are hated. The usual reason given is that their burrows break cattle and horse legs, though the scientific veracity of this claim is debatable. Studies from Colorado State University indicate that prairie dogs can actually increase cattle yields, because burrowing aerates soils, leading moisture to the parched earth and grass.

Despite this, the creatures face extermination by methods that include drowning, dynamiting, burrow ripping, and bait poisoning. One man, who goes by Mr. Dog, profiled by *Mother Jones*, said he preferred a Remington .222. Mr. Dog claimed to have bulleted seventy-five straight once before missing.

I think in meeting Watson, I wanted to talk with somebody who could help illuminate why the mass of people would have such a hating bias toward a thing, when others would crawl out of the same burrow, the same town, the same Lubbock, with a completely different view.

My story, though Lynda Watson said she wasn't interested in it, is that I'm a former owner of a prairie dog and also grew up in Lubbock. The late 1990s and early 2000s were interesting times to own a prairie dog in West Texas. In addition to all the fumigating and varmint hunting, in 2003 the CDC and FDA banned prairie dogs as pets, and the city of Lubbock began killing scores of dogs because it was convinced, erroneously, that the rodents were responsible for poisoning ground water.

I gave my prairie dog the ironic name Squirrel, and her friendly attitude didn't disappoint. She was about the size of two fists, short-fuzzed, mouse-smelling, vocal. She greeted me after school every day from her six-foot-tall cage with a rearing on hind legs, followed by a high-pitched "whir whoh!" squeal, reminiscent of two plucked violin strings. Biologists call this the prairie dog's "jump yip." It's the sound Squirrel greeted me with for nine years. She welcomed me from pubescence until I was in my twenties.

As with most adolescents, my keeping a mammalian life allowed me to practice the awkwardness of social-biological kinships. Squirrel's comfort elbowed me out of quotidian anxieties, made it hard to hold a too-harsh view of the universe. It's difficult to be spiteful for long when an animated fur-squeak-toy wants to crawl up your leg and go to sleep on your lap.

I'd mentioned on the phone to Lynda that I once cared for a prairie dog, and I laid bare my bias, hoping to share a kind of interspecies bond. A quick Google search will reveal all the ways to kill them, the proper poisons, the gun ranges where people have fur targets instead of paper. But it's rare to find another person attached as I was. And in Lynda's gruff way of saying, after we'd hung out, "You don't seem so terrible," I think she came to see that we did have a similar outlook, though my hands were far less scarred than hers.

Sixty prairie dogs are cooped inside Lynda's skylit shed, which, when we walk in, smells like cat meal processed with mold. Three rows of cages stand against a wall. The prairie dogs flutter like birds about the mesh. Wood shavings and turds kick into the air. As I near a larger animal, it rears on its haunches and lets out a "whir whoh!" squeal that sends a jolt of memory through me.

Lynda pries open a cage and tosses in a plate of chopped carrots, cucumbers, and radishes. Some animals scurry from her hand, while others hunch and eat—one feasting as Lynda strokes its back. "They do make good pets," she agrees.

As we leave, Lynda switches on a radio hanging from the wall. A Nashville crooner pops from the speakers. "As long as it's not religious, I think they like it," she says.

We walk to Lynda's Chevy Silverado parked in the dusty and mesquite-shaded expanse of a backyard. Hitched to the truck is a trailer hauling a rusty five-hundred-gallon tank. The tank is leaking water as if bladder-shot. The truck bed is filled with cages, a cooler of bottled water, and dish soap.

Why soap? Bubbles, Lynda tells me, panic the prairie dogs into thinking they're drowning before they actually are. She gauges that the soap isn't healthy, but neither is drowning or extermination.

While we're talking, Lynda's assistant, Luke, wheels up to join. He is six feet tall with a beer belly, soft voice, and pale goatee. Luke made friends with Lynda thirty years ago and has worked for her since retiring, scooping up prairie dogs and driving.

"I can't sit around all day watching TV," Luke says. "My retirement is catching prairie dogs."

He claims he's seen Lynda give mouth-to-mouth to a waterlogged prairie dog by wrapping her lips around its snout. He says, shaking his head in disbelief at the memory, "She's the prairie dog guru. Nobody knows more about prairie dogs than she does."

As I read on the front page of the *Lubbock Avalanche-Journal*, a year after prairie dogs were banned by the CDC, when George W. Bush won reelection, my hometown of Lubbock in 2004 was in the country's second most conservative county by votes. If I may weave a dangerous blanket statement from growing up in this culture, one that currently enjoys a political winning streak, it's that people of this persuasion do not often take to wildlife. And when they do, it is often to shoot them.

This, I think, stems partly from vestiges of Puritanism—that witch-hunting, scarlet-letter-sewing, violent belief in perfection. Puritanism is destructive because it defines purity by what it is not, and privileges the absence of defilers. One's soul, home, and environment must be kept clean, sinners and prairie dogs wiped out, despite whatever suffering this might incur.

Puritanical animus is not restricted to prairie dogs. David Baron, in his book *Beast in the Garden*, catalogs the history of Americans' bloody confrontation with creatures coast to coast. Predators are well known for driving men to guns, politicians to poisons. So much lay outside of rural Americans' control: the weather, soil, microbes. Predator hunts or prairie dog burrow dynamiting were within sway.

I'm not sure how much has changed. So much of life seems beyond reason. Other creatures can receive pent-up hostility because they cannot communicate back. Even my us/them setup, I admit, is a remnant of Puritanism, my frustrations with my hometown.

Except that some people, like Lynda, seem to have been able to hear prairie dogs and understand their jump yips. Lynda, living in the same community as many prairie dog enemies, now takes it as her mission to save as many as she can. Not only is she a random fragment, she's a contradiction.

West of Lubbock lies a now-closed air force base turned community college, truck driving school, hovercraft testing site, and technology center. The administrators decided a few years ago that all animals were welcome on its grassy property, provided they didn't overrun the place, which they have.

Lynda reaches across her dash for one of a half dozen passes to show to the uniformed attendant at the barrier.

"They must trust you a lot," I say.

She shrugs. "They have to; I'm the only one who does this."

As we drive up, it looks like everything has run amok on the base besides mammals. Old barracks stand with broken windows and collapsed, rotten roofs. The grass is ankle deep in sage, swarmed by mating dragonflies. An antiquated air traffic control tower leans and suffers vines spiraling up its paint-chipped stairs.

Last year, Lynda spotted eagles out here, four or five species of fox, coyotes, skunks, raccoons, and burrowing owls, which can't exist without tunnels to live in dug by prairie dogs.

Lynda aims a finger at a foot-tall burrowing owl standing sentry over its bunker. "There's a whole family there, living like they're supposed to," she says as we drive around, the sun glowing over everything, the grass lining up like the military once housed here. Beaming at the wild, Lynda looks content, stoic, her skin a deep tan, her eyes aimed at the ground.

As the world's most famous prairie dog catcher, Lynda has received armadas of press coverage and, for a short time (I guess true for everyone) minor celebrity status in Japan.

What is amazing to me, among a list of fantastic attributes you could apply to Lynda Watson, is her level of success in the misogynist world of ranching. Before rodents, Lynda mastered the art of breaking horses, training mules, and trading livestock. All before dropping out of junior high.

She was born in 1954 as Lynda Hatfield on a thirty-acre farm outside Lansing, Michigan. Her eyes were rolled back into their sockets, entailing corrective surgery and a lifetime of bad vision. In utero, her cheekbones narrowed the shape of her mouth, leaving no room for incisors. Ironically, these are the same teeth that prairie dogs grow throughout their lives, and use to gnaw grass and sometimes Lynda's hands.

Lynda had two alcoholic parents who held door-slamming, oath-taking, glass-smashing, all-night fights. She describes her youth as "redneck," "blue collar," and "trash." She says that her clothes reeked, and because her daddy was a hunting guide, he would be absent from their trailer for long stretches.

Outside of attending school and training horses, Lynda trapped small animals. Many, she said, she let go. I hazard this is where her understanding grew, a kinship with something small, trying to survive, broken by circumstance.

After dropping out of school, Lynda married at sixteen. She admitted her husband was an escape, as marriages often can be in such cases. Her husband was a military man who got shipped to Reese Air Base in Lubbock, the same one where she would later let me tag along.

Lynda became pregnant on base and had a son, but he died nine months later with the same defects Lynda had been born with. She divorced her husband when she realized his drunken abuse was just what she'd tried to leave behind.

Lynda hated Texas at first: the heat, the barrenness, the dust sweeping in through shut windows and piling in drifts. The dryness. But, divorced, she had to work and had experience only with animals. She groomed dogs. She worked on feedlots and was fired because she refused to conform to stereotype and lechery. She drank a lot of whiskey.

At some point she met an ancient trapper who still caught rodents with his hands, a dying, almost extinguished breed even in the 1970s. This trapper had the idea to begin selling the furry creatures as pets.

Lynda fires a cigarette with one of the many lighters scattered across the dash of her truck. Luke pops a curb, dragging the water-tank trailer behind him onto the unkempt grass. Several micro-volcanos erupt from earth, and with them barking prairie dogs.

Lynda cracks the door and runs out of the moving truck. She does this because the rodents escape to the deepest parts of the den when her truck rumbles over. She jogs behind a burrow and raises a fist when the trailer's water tank is in position. Luke crushes the brake. In back, Lynda drops to her knees, padded by a slice of turquoise foam. She pries open the tank's water spout, and the flood begins.

Luke squeezes amber soap from a bottle into the stream. Lynda leans back, bracing her hands at the opening, stretched like a spider spanning a hole. She waits, foam bubbling. She tells me later she can read the bubbles and know when a prairie dog is about to surface.

One does, panicked. Snake-quick, Lynda fires her hand at the dog's throat, pinching its jaws closed. The bundle twitches and kicks in a fur tornado. Lynda hands the rodent to Luke, who grabs the tail. He dangles the animal head down, draining the soap. The dog goes still, zonked. Luke drops the soaked critter into a cage in front of the water tank while Lynda waits for another rodent to emerge.

A thousand miles away and fifteen years ago, a pet seller in Illinois commingled a sick Gambian rat with a supply of for-sale American prairie dogs, which were sold to customers in Wisconsin. A few prairie dog owners became ill with monkeypox.

Monkeypox is about what you'd think: a smallpox-like virus transmitted through fluid contact with infected mammals. Signs include engorged lymph nodes, a lumpy, scaling rash on the face, crusty, spreading lesions on extremities. Possible death. No known cure.

Until 2003 it had never been seen outside Africa, which is why it was strange when a dozen prairie dog owners in the Midwest became bedridden. Who could predict that a grassland-loving rodent would have picked up a virus from the rain forests of Cameroon?

In June 2003, discovering the prairie dog connection, the CDC recommended that all Americans avoid any contact with prairie dogs that appeared ill. On June 11 the CDC and FDA issued a joint "immediate embargo" on the sale, transportation, and release of prairie dogs and other "certain rodents" (but not monkeys).

This ban was arguably irrational because native prairie dogs have as much chance of contracting the sub-Saharan disease as any other rodent or primate or dog. But one effect was to kill the pet prairie dog trade, including Lynda Watson's. Overnight, Walter's World of Pets in Lubbock, where I'd bought Squirrel, went from selling two hundred prairie dogs a year to zero. Many sellers resorted to killing their charges.

The next dog Lynda pulls out dripping reveals a red abscess on the side of its throat, acorn sized. Like people, prairie dogs sometimes need medical attention, so Lynda keeps a large med kit in the back of her truck. She washes her hands with dish soap while Luke dangles the critter. Retrieving a razor and antibiotic, she lances the boil, out of which pours a coffee-and-cream-colored geyser of pus.

"I can smell that," Luke says, as rotten meat scent hits our noses.

The creature is silent as Lynda lathers it with oily antibiotic. She tells me she often finds wounds from unsuccessful hawks and still-hungry coyotes.

After catching a dozen prairie dogs, Lynda and Luke drive to the second location of the day, one of Lubbock's elementary schools. The school has been "a monumental job," according to Lynda. She has already removed hundreds of prairie dogs from the pock-marked schoolyard. All that are left are difficult animals, gun shy. "It's getting to the point," she says, "where I'm going to have to say that some need to be poisoned because I can't get them." She puffs on her cigarette. "So, my approach today is no more Mr. Nice Guy."

At the school, Lynda employs field glasses like a battlefield commander. She chain-smokes, sighting prairie dogs that scurry across the lawn. Dragonflies buzz around with the hum of a highway nearby.

Lynda picks out her prey and hops in the cab, yelling at Luke to drive. After the truck rolls up the curb and drags the water tank over a burrow, Lynda jumps out, cigarette in hand, signals Luke to stop, swivels the water on. She pours in Dial, then grabs a cage from the trailer and holds it open against the tunnel.

There is a crashing of furred body against metal trap. The critter pops into the cage and bangs and squeezes against the side. Lynda pulls the cage back and reaches a blind hand into the sudsy fluid where the dog is deciding whether to surface or drown. She makes that decision easier by lassoing its neck.

At the next hole, Lynda fists one and retrieves. As she's passing it to Luke, the dog's teeth clamp onto the soft tissue of her right thumb. She cries, "Get him! Shit!" Luke scoops up the dog, but not before rodent teeth draw Lynda's skin away, a jet of blood pumping out.

"Is it bad?" Luke asks.

"The worst part is the nausea," She says. "That's how you know it's bad."

Quickly she trots to the med kit and pops it open to find gauze and antiseptic. After a quick rinse, she tapes the gauze tightly to the wound.

"I get bit four or five times a year," she says, and later points to scars covering both of her arms. "If it was on my left hand, I could stitch this up myself, but since it's not, I'll have to get my vet to do it for me."

Her worst injury, she tells me later, was when a prairie dog latched onto her pinky finger and spun around, the skin peeling off like tape. "That made me really, really sick," she says. Moments like that, she forgets she's trying to save them.

———

I am lucky enough to see Lynda rescue twenty-five prairie dogs. Some days, she tells me, they can't save any. I'll get a glimpse of this boom-bust cycle at their third and final location of the day, another elementary school on the far north side of town, surrounded by cotton fields. There, despite a yard lesioned with burrows, Lynda and Luke can't capture a single rodent. Lynda's thumb throbs; the Texas heat climbs to 105. She calls it quits.

Lynda shields her customers, 85 percent of whom, she says, make her sign a confidential disclosure agreement because they don't wish neighbors to know that they harbor rodents. I want to see the results of her work, though, and Lynda informs me that one great success, open to the public, is Caprock Canyons State Park. It lies two hours northeast of Lubbock. She gives me the number of a park ranger there.

I say goodbye to her and Luke and give my thanks. The last time I see Lynda Watson, she waves from the pickup, firing another cigarette, the water tank covered in dust still leaking behind them, twenty-five just-rescued prairie dogs jumping and chirping in cages, drying in the sun as they're wheeled to a new home.

Caprock Canyons State Park reveals millions of years of sandstone usually invisible, lying beneath the tabletop-flat terrain of the Llano Estacado. The park also hosts the Texas State Bison Herd, recently released to roam the park, along with rescued prairie dogs.

Ranger Chester Losey Hawkins helped Lynda relocate the prairie dogs. He goes by C.L. and is a fourth-generation West Texas rancher. His family still owns land adjacent to the park where they raise cattle. He is fifty-one, square-shouldered, eyes carved into a permanent squint, and has been a Texas Parks employee for twenty-two years.

This year has been the busiest season in C.L.'s memory, largely due to the bison and prairie dogs. His work-issued Ford F-150 is littered with the usual paperwork, maps, and air fresheners, along with a backseat piled with Chinese lanterns. "Found at a campsite," he explains. "We find all kinds of cool stuff that people leave behind, and we try to recycle it."

Seeing those lanterns, and remembering Lynda Watson's "Recycle Prairie Dogs" shirt, something strikes me about recycling. In essence, Lynda and C.L. are helping the feedback loops that define ecosystems, reusing life and nonlife.

To import the prairie dogs that Lynda rescued, C.L. drove out here first with a tractor mower and leveled the field. Then the trick was, he tells me, to not release and scatter the prairie dogs. He kept them in a wire cage anchored to the ground, open to the soil. To escape, the prairie dogs had to dig their way out. They constructed a new home.

We follow a dirt road and overlook a steep drop of perhaps three hundred feet into a switchback of the canyon, a majestic view of buttes, sandstone, scrub, and deep red rock. Beside the epic view, a new colony is set up. The prairie dog town is the size of a football field, bordered by an RV camp and tall grass.

Witnessing the colony is akin to watching a day care center or dog park, a swirling mass of busy adorable life. Prairie dogs jump-yip, root. They chase and shovel dirt. I look over and see C.L. smiling, and I can't help it too.

"We still have our doubters," he says, "but the overwhelming majority of comments, especially from children, has been positive."

As C.L. drives me around, he reveals that rescuing the prairie dogs was not his idea. "My father didn't like prairie dogs," he says. "Neither did my grandfather, my great-grandfather. It was hard for me not to hate them, growing up that way."

I ask him what made him change his mind. He mentions a rodent that lost her right front leg, named Tripod by the rangers. She had a litter of puppies, and rangers would take turns watching her, reporting on her children. Tripod could sit on her haunches and eat with one arm, scooping food in one paw. She took care of her pups and made regular appearances to visitors. Then one day, no Tripod. Coyote, hawk, rattlesnake, erratic driver, or disease.

"It was sad to lose old Tripod," C.L. says with what appears to be a tremor. "She had character. Things like that will make you love these creatures. When they become people to you."

It may be difficult to distinguish rodents, as if they had voices, but prairie dogs have the most sophisticated language ever decoded, according to scientists. Even better than orcas or dolphins.

Researchers at the University of Northern Arizona, after years studying colony chatter, found that prairie dog calls are so complex, they not only differentiate species (coyote versus dog) but even communicate details, such as pink shirt or green, Labrador or German shepherd.

Something about this language sophistication makes me recall my own experience with Squirrel. I remember her adorable "whir whoh!" as I came in the door, and again as I stepped into the room, and as I opened her six-foot cage. She would rear back on her hind legs, bob up, call, and sink back down. Each time, I felt a warm ember in my chest but also the irony that, I thought, her jump-yip was meant to be threatening.

But now it seems unclear what the jump-yip is for. Prairie dog towns have waves of yipping, the original yippers stopping to forage, yips changing when a hawk's shadow passes. The jump-yip seems ineffectual as territorial bark. Instead it seems like a checking in.

This explanation isn't clear, but I like adopting it. I like thinking that Squirrel, when I came home, my thoughts filled with zings of adolescence, was telling me it was okay to sit down, because she was watching.

One of my fondest memories is of Squirrel slipping out of her cage at night and curling up in a ball the size of a human heart to lie on my bare chest without my noticing until I woke up to find her purring. She was never sick until the spring of 2007, when she got what I thought was an ordinary cold. My college roommate found her stiff while I was out of town, and we buried her in the backyard. I cried more over her funeral than I did for my own grandmother's.

Squirrel's death and learning about Tripod's make me recall the ideas of conservationist Aldo Leopold, when he wrote that people grieve what they know, or what they can communicate with. Rodents seem like alien life-forms, but only from a distance.

Maybe, I admit, like the way I look at election maps and make judgments.

The work establishing the new colonies was not hard, C.L. says, just he and Lynda, about four other park employees, and a tractor auger. The only time the rescued critters were fed was the first year, because of drought. Then, Lynda drove in with a load of sweet potatoes.

C.L. pulls the truck into a way-in-the-back primitive camping site and tells me a story. About fifteen years ago, he crossed the fenceless land between his property and the park, dressed in camouflage. He shouldered a rifle for hunting and binoculars. As he topped the hill overlooking the canyon, he espied a group of teenagers, "hippie-looking with long hair," he says, "smoking weed." C.L. found it glorious to spy on these lawbreakers, to know that he was looking down on a group that had no idea they were being watched.

I startled and laughed, because it easily could have been me and my friends back then, escaping Lubbock. I had long hair from the time I graduated from Lubbock High, and ignited large quantities of marijuana. I found it charming—something about the possible encounter and reencounter with C.L. We shared in the laughter and joy of nosing into the privacy of delinquents, knowing that our worlds, urban and rural, were so much closer than we might have made out, than the culture defines, than is a part of binary discourse. The land connected his experiences and mine, like prairie dog tunnels linked unseen underground. Lynda Watson wasn't so much a contradiction as a revelation of the falsehood of cultural and interspecies divisions.

When I was a teenager, I treated the land above the canyon's crest as the boundary of the earth, just as I often catch myself, with someone who differs from me, wrongly drawing them in my mind as my enemy. The vestiges of Puritanism are as strong in conservatives and liberals and ranchers and environmentalists and me. But all it took for C.L. was working in a park that imported prairie dogs and becoming affected by a three-legged mother. All it took for me was talking with him. Perceptions alter, animals can change in the minds of their beholders just like with people and their ideas of themselves.

Our worlds are connected by ecotones where our memories and personalities blend into indistinguishable features. C.L. remembers stumbling upon a group of pot-smoking hippies. I recall being enthralled by a landscape where I mistakenly thought I was all alone.

Evolving the Monster
A HISTORY OF GODZILLA

The first monster movie I ever saw was Godzilla, and I remember the moment like one does a trauma. Age six, curled up on my parents' bed, lights black, using the only VCR in the house. This was the sole time I would be scared of the atomic dragon. The only night Godzilla would sneak into my sleep and chase me down the highways and dark train lines of Tokyo.

Godzilla engrossed me the way Jaws and Alligator did, even as they seeded a paranoia against swimming that bled into adulthood. As a kid, I remember fear, the thrill of imagining things that lurked beneath the carpet, or behind my walls, or hovering above my bedroom. The books I read, the stories I was told, the real beasts I encountered. Once, I was nipped on the ass by an aunt's Doberman and later begged my parents for one. Still today, If I'm in the mood for horror, it's for monster films that unzip my skin in a sheet.

Godzilla holds the Guinness world record for longest continually run film franchise: thirty-one movies over sixty-three years. In 2015, a poll revealed Godzilla was the most popular monster among Americans, ahead of Frankenstein's creature and our claymation Kong. The monster we are most fascinated with is known for ripping up metropolises on the far side of the ocean. What bright flame has drawn our imaginations toward a creature that destroys lives on the other side of the sea?

Godzilla was born in 1954 and has accomplished much in his life. In film, he has traveled to Osaka, Shanghai, New York, Sydney, Hong

Kong, Honolulu, Tokyo many times, Sapporo, San Francisco, and Antarctica. He's encountered and defeated a three-headed dragon, a giant bloodsucking dragonfly, a moth goddess, a giant condor, a giant spider, a robot version of himself, another robot version of himself, a monster made out of sludge, a monster controlled by aliens who are really cockroaches, a monster controlled by aliens from the third planet near the black hole, and a monster that is a giant plant made out of radioactive cells, rose petals, and the soul of a botanist's murdered daughter.

Besides roaring, stomping, crushing, and roasting, he has learned many skills. He has danced, meditated, and sprinted. He has dived, swum, and navigated lava tubes. He has learned how to digest nuclear reactors. He has cracked an iceberg like a walnut. He's played volleyball with a boulder and a giant lobster. He's learned to parent his son. He's managed to talk with his friends. And, using atomic breath as propulsion, he has even managed to fly.

The Godzilla movies after 1954's *Gojira* were not about radiation or environmental ethics. The films morphed from sequel ripoff to monster battles to Godzilla acting as Tokyo guard-dog pummeling *kaiju* that rumbled close. Godzilla movies, after the first, are about awe, which is something children understand, that primal satisfaction of seeing the world's limits stretched past their breaking, watching horizons spread.

Writing now, I must acknowledge that inner six-year-old who has long been attracted to things outside his horizons, the primal corpus of psychology who cranes his neck at clouds and skyscrapers and marvels at food piles at state fairs, who visits zoos and gawks at bears. Godzilla films—I've watched all thirty-one—entrance me not because the plots are complicated or the special effects avant-garde, but because they ask me to feed my ravenous imagination.

I have little practice in film criticism but a lot more writing about invasive species. I think my flirtation with invasives stems from my childhood monster-wonder.

In trying to figure out Godzilla, watching all of the movies and researching the bibliography, I've come to see him as the ultimate invasive species. Not man-made but man-morphed, something that's been around but nudged with human tinkering into menace, reminding us of what we've done.

As an ecological being, Godzilla's niche is deep-ocean apex predator. He stands 50 meters tall, or 100 or 118.5 meters, depending on the movie. Godzilla was ripped from his ecology by nuclear radiation that the United States scattered across the Ring of Fire. The beast grew, inherited nuclear capabilities, and was driven from his home by the same spark of light that birthed his terrifying breath.

His skin is charcoal ash gray, sometimes evergreen, and tough: withstanding bullets, bombs, lasers. In one movie, scientists studying Godzilla debate the medical advances to be made from skin that can shrug off tank shells. One of the scientists worries that if the military murders the monster, Godzilla science will be lost forever. The creature is a walking rain forest, shielding its mysteries, lumbering with possibility.

That the discovery of Godzilla bears the cost of destruction, cities laid waste so human knowledge may lurch forward, harkens to an ancient, carnal, biblical transaction. Something akin to growing up.

When I was nine, I received my first Godzilla action figure from a rich aunt who lived in a pillared mansion on Ocean Drive in Corpus Christi. The toy was eighteen inches tall, muscled, snarling, with tough plastic-leather skin. I played with this toy more than any other, Godzilla winning his battles, toppling a model of my aunt's house made out of Legos, a house she prized. The house where once I stayed, sprinting up staircases, tornadoing around the gaudy halls and epic backyard. Where I broke a window and remember no punishment. Where one of her three guard-dog Dobermans bit my ass. A place where I had enough space to exhibit my monstrous self.

Godzilla was the toy I most identified with as a macho-raised male, the aggressive element of steam-valve destruction (my aunt's window a victim).

Besides Godzilla, I also grew up with 1980s action heroes: Rambo, Van Damme, Arnold. I replayed their films over and over on our VCR, gawking at the terrifying muscles erupting from skin. The harm they could cause, their power over the Earth. Maybe that is what I hated, as a kid, the lack of control; I envied action-star agency. Possibly I also craved the giant space of my aunt's, as if I were a creature alone in the world.

Hollywood action heroes, I realize now, were another kind of monster, morphing the human form through weights and steroids and retrograde masculine tropes. And they too left destruction in other countries across distant seas.

On March 1, 1954, the tuna trawler Lucky Dragon 5 was sailing the Pacific off the Marshall Islands. Twenty-three sailors witnessed a light appearing on the horizon, shimmering, then glowing, then blinding. One claimed later he saw "the sun rising in the west." A seven-thousand-square-mile mushroom sprouted, and ash rained on their faces.

In port, the sailors were diagnosed with radiation poisoning and burns on exposed skin. The radio operator would soon die of liver failure. The fish in the ship's hold were radioactive, as were subsequent catches. Emperor Hirohito, appalled, said he would cease eating fish, and many citizens followed—this in an island country synonymous with sushi. Japanese journalists dubbed it "Japan's third atomic strike."

Two weeks after the Bikini Atoll hydrogen bomb test, film producer Tomoyuki Tanaka commuted over the Pacific. His latest film project scrapped, he was mulling his failure and the new power unleashed onto the world. He fretted as he looked out the plane, at the horizon-cracking blue, knowing about the radiation entering the water that surrounds Japan like a death hand.

For Japan the ocean has long been ominous, the bringer of tsunamis, hurricanes, Americans. Peering over the fathomlessness of the atomic-wracked Pacific, Tanaka wondered, what could be down there that humans were awakening?

———

The original Gojira of 1954 is not to be confused with the castrated, imbecilic Godzilla, King of the Monsters! starring Raymond Burr. The latter replaced almost a third of the Japanese cinematic marvel with footage shot in one marathon twenty-four-hour filming session, and dubbing that took just four hours.

Gojira's antinuclear message was clipped, as was the hand-wringing by one of the scientists about whether to use an even worse weapon, the Oxygen Destroyer, to liquify Godzilla. The slashed footage hints that Japanese scientists codeveloped the Oxygen Destroyer with Germans during the war but decided, unlike Americans with their atoms, not to unleash that weapon on the world.

No, in the American version the scientists have fewer scruples about using their weapons, less guilt for the destruction they cause. Power, the American version seems to say, is not made to be chained.

Tanaka's Gojira begins idyllically: sweaty yet smiling sailors aboard a fishing vessel, the men guitar-strumming and harmonica-humming. Then a bright flash, the men rushing to the deck. Water boiling. The sailors scream as the light grows to surface-of-the-sun hot. The ship erupts in flames. There is a shot of the guitar alone on deck, abandoned, burning. Innocence and youth ablaze.

During Gojira's production, the director, Ishiro Honda, added the detail of Godzilla's atomic breath. Honda had survived Tokyo's firebombing, only to be shipped out to China as a soldier. When he repatriated, he traveled through Hiroshima, and he witnessed the nuclear aftermath. He wrote, "There was a heavy atmosphere . . . a fear the world was already coming to an end." When filming attack scenes, Honda remembered the Tokyo bomb attack, people looking up and watching fire rain.

Honda desired a monster that didn't simply lumber and cause random damage like an excited dog. Atomic breath gave Godzilla agency. He could melt tanks, decapitate skyscrapers, poison a nation's fish. Isotopes from his glowing head were what humans had cocreated with the ancient world.

Gojira's score composer, Akira Ifukube, also suffered radiation poisoning during the war. He would compose eleven of the Godzilla film scores as well as scores for two hundred other movies. He was also tasked with creating Godzilla's roar. He wanted something natural and ethereal, organic but metallic, the sound of the deep ocean as well as the psychic vibrations of monster mythology.

He visited Tokyo's Music Conservatory, which housed the only contrabass in the nation. With permission, Ifukube donned a leather glove and gripped and slid his hand down the bass strings. He recorded the sound and put an echo to the recording. What resulted was a roar that would reverberate sixty years into the stomachs of Japanese and Americans, into children across every ocean, waking arm hairs, reconfiguring memories of war and animal gods, alerting us to the living mysteries lying beyond and beneath our horizons.

Among sixty years of unfathomable creations in the Godzilla universe, one stands out: Hedorah, the smog monster. In 1971's *Godzilla vs. the Smog Monster*, Hedorah congeals from pollution boiling in Tokyo Bay. The creature is reminiscent of a child's trash-bag ghost costume with blood eyes spraying lightning bolts and excreting toxic sludge. Hedorah first swims as a mutated tadpole. Then he stalks on land and finally flies on his own flatulence. His emissions melt people, breaking down bodies into skeletons.

At one point Hedorah wraps his gray lips around an industrial chimney and *tokes*. His eyes roll back, and the smog creature appears giddy until quarrelsome Godzilla roars.

During the fight, Hedorah fires a snotball at Godzilla that burns his shoulder. Godzilla later repays him by punching out his eye. Godzilla then falls into a cavernous hole, into which Hedorah pours what appears to be toxic excreta.

In the film's most bizarre scene, the young male character, Yukio, freaks out, it seems, on LSD in an underground dance club. Yukio is decked in skinny peach pants and leopard shirt, moping at a table while his girlfriend dances and sings in a catsuit to a song called "Give Me Back My Planet."

Yukio is staring at his girlfriend, at all the other go-go dancers, when suddenly the room spins, darkens, and everyone's face is replaced with a fish head. Yukio sweats, panics, screams, and the lights come back on. Then a river of Hedorah sludge descends the stairs. The party bellows, melts, or escapes, the lava lamps shining. Having had bad acid trips, I empathize with Yukio and his vertiginous confluence of hallucination and toxic reality. It makes me wonder if the movie creators harbored a sadism toward teenagers, as Hollywood slasher films do. It's unfair, berating teenagers for being young, while most of them, if my life is any indication, don't appreciate their youth and won't until skin begins peeling, just like the people Hedorah melts with his sludge.

There are other theories for the success of monster films besides awesomeness and sadism. One, of course, is that monster movies project our fears that we will destroy the Earth and our guilt over doing so. Another is that Godzilla precipitates the violent catharsis that action movies always perform, and before them quest novels and Gilgamesh.

More disturbing to me are film historian Frank Dello Stritto's arguments about the sexuality of monster stories, in the book *A Quaint & Curious Volume of Forgotten Lore: The Mythology & History of Classic Horror Films*. In his theory, a more-than-human interloper enters a socially oppressive atmosphere, acts on forbidden cravings, and attempts to combat ruling norms. Monster stories, in this view, are voyeuristic, and they reward traditions that keep monsters thwarted: the Church, with its ability to stake transgressors, and the military and scientists for neutralizing radioactive beasts.

But the theory I'm more fond of comes from David Quammen in his book *Monster of God*. The enduring success of beasts, from Grendel to *Alien*, Quammen writes, "reflects not just our fear of homicidal monsters but also our need and desire for them. . . . They allow us to recollect our limitations. They keep us company. The universe is a very big place, but as far as we know it's mainly empty, boring, and cold."

As a child I had an obsessive fear that I would be alone when my parents died. That I would never marry, that it would be as hard to make friends in adulthood as in childhood. Having Godzilla, the lone isolated predator, gave me a kind of kinship. Someone else, a fellow misfit.

For almost every Toho Godzilla film until the 1990s, a new suit was handcrafted. I noticed this as a child: the crocodilian look in *Godzilla vs. King Kong*, the buck teeth of *Godzilla Raids Again*, the punched-up acne scarring in *Son of Godzilla*.

Similarly, Godzilla has meant something different to me through my life, from the terror when I was six, to a friend when I was nine, to an amusement and, currently, a curiosity.

In metaphor, Godzilla has morphed from nuclear parable to pollution PSA in Smog Monster to a projection of Japanese nationalism in *Shin Gojira*, which followed the 2011 tsunami, earthquake, and subsequent nuclear meltdown at Fukushima. In *Shin Gojira*, Godzilla slithers up a canal, exploding Tokyo's rivers, crushing boats in a gargle of foam and mud that spills onto shore. The scene recalls the myriad public-captured moments of the tsunami, when the ocean raised a battering fist.

Politicians in the movie are as inept as in 2011, lying to the public, meeting for mind-chilling hours, resolving little. Then Americans want to drop a nuke, their fourth nuclear strike. The movie advocates resistance to big-brother interference, to Americans who begot the creature. The monster isn't Godzilla but bureaucracy thrust upon the island nation, another kind of human-natural disaster.

The original Godzilla design was a giant octopus, but producer Tomoyuki Tanaka scrapped this. He helped evolve Godzilla into the T-rex-stegosaurus-dragon hybrid we know. Bamboo stakes and chicken wire were overlaid with urethane and latex and bulky padding, a suit with zero ventilation.

During filming, monster stuntman Haruo Nakajima fainted inside his suit, crushing city miniatures before cue. The crew wrapped in August with sizzling lights. Three minutes was the max the actor could take inside Godzilla. During breaks, grips unsuited Nakajima and poured out a cup of his sweat. He lost twenty pounds during filming.

Before shooting, Nakajima worried about how to play his part. How does one portray a lumbering monster who is half dinosaur and half nuclear reactor, part myth and part human foible? How does one become a beast who, like a child, seems to crave destruction but is yet not fully responsible for his monstrousness?

For inspiration, Nakajima visited the Ueno Zoo, where he sat outside bear pens and watched grizzlies lumber around. These natural monsters were confined too, twisted by their human habitation.

I visited this same zoo when I lived in Japan as an English teacher, and I remember the bears well. I was struck by one who paced his cage, bellowing nonstop. The size of the real-life bear rippling before me snapped my brain. A part of me did not think bears were possible; from watching them on television, they looked to be filmmaker creations.

It was because I had been conditioned since I was six by Godzilla, the films mushrooming bears into radioactive monsters and setting them loose upon my imagination. Godzilla evolved the way I look at life. Why I go to zoos. Why, on some level, I want the animals to be bigger. And why I want them to escape.

For 2016's *Shin Gojira*, Toho Studios didn't hire a sweaty man in a suit, but rather a green screen studio and motion-capture technology. Toho abandoned stuntmen and chose a fifty-year-old Noh actor to play the beast.

Noh is an eight-century-old masked theatre tradition, a slow, rhythmic, patient shifting of the limbs in yogalike dances that can last for hours. The actor Mansai Nomura morphed Godzilla from slouching beast to ponderous dancer cutting a methodical path through Tokyo.

In an interview, Nomura said that Noh "isn't even human. It's godlike, ghostlike, even monsterlike . . . heavy and lumbering. For the role, I even used a Godzilla mask just to understand . . . When Godzilla stomps Tokyo, I could really see him acting the Noh." After sixty years, Nomura helped update the beast. Like any creature who survives for long, Godzilla keeps evolving, a human product born from animal impulses, lying beneath the surface but also trudging through the art of creation.

The Great Story of the
Stinking Cedar in the Garden of Eden

The Florida torreya, known as the stinking cedar, is a 165-million-year-old yew species.

It is older than *Tyrannosaurus rex*. It is older than tree sloths, alligators, whale sharks, and bees. It is older than the Bering Sea, Hawai'i, half of Australia, and the dwarf planet Pluto.

It is called "stinking" for the musk of celery, tomato, and turpentine that wafts to your nose when you sniff its needles. Its seeds, after they fall, have the uncanny ability of mimicking raw sewage.

The evolutionary theory is that the seeds were consumed by roaming Paleolithic behemoths, carried in the gullets of shit-loving mastodons and spectacled bears and giant sloths, spread to new homes upon digestion.

One ecologist estimated that there were six hundred thousand stinking cedars in Florida before the twentieth century. By 1950, most were harvested for fence posts, shingles, and Christmas trees. Stinking cedars perfumed bungalows. Shingles kept living rooms warm while stinking cedar planks fenced and guarded yards. Children unwrapped Christmas presents scented with turpentine. The trees wove in and out of Floridians' lives, creating the bulwark for their passage through time.

Minus colossal Paleolithic carriers, hunted out by early Americans, stinking cedars are restricted to where their golfball seeds fall. And because of climate change, a pathogen previously unknown to science is slaughtering torreya newborns. As the warming planet's heat laps at their branches, the once-verdant needles are shading to the color of rust.

With all these changes, there are as few as six hundred stinking cedars left in the world. Six hundred, of one of the oldest of Earth's living things.

Some humans are constructing a lifeboat for the creature, an exodus from the extinction we're causing. This journey may carry us away into a different story about our relationship with nature, a story with several characters, one that heralds the death of Eden and doesn't mourn.

A not-for-profit group of citizens, the Torreya Guardians, have gathered saplings and seeds of stinking cedars and shipped them to more than thirty locations around the world. They fret the species will wink out, and so they are Fed-Exing its progeny to backyard refuges.

Through Skype, I managed to contact the Torreya Guardians' president, Connie Barlow, who also works as a traveling preacher with her husband. For a living, the couple preach not Christ but the gospel of Darwin. They address astronomy and ecology and archaeology at prisons, libraries, schools, Catholic and Unitarian churches. They are self-proclaimed "evolutionary evangelicals" who live in a van, journeying the North American continent.

They drive and park, lecture under crucifixes, flanked by bars or stained glass windows, and reveal the formation of all being from what has come before. The constant rearranging of atoms and DNA into mesmerizing new forms, an odyssey of biology.

"Tell me," Connie says, "a story more wondrous than that of a living cell forged from the residue of exploding stars. Or a transformation more magical than a fish falling out onto land. Or a myth more compelling than a reptile taking to the air and becoming a bird or a mammal slipping back into the sea and becoming a whale."

This is the cosmic tale of deep time swirling in the supernovas and condensing into the first microbe, tree, salamander, and human, the wheel of spark and death, the ongoing saga of our collective journey that they call "The Great Story."

In 2003, during a break from evangelical wandering, Connie was strolling Torreya State Park in North Florida, where the last stinking cedars are. She searched for the park's namesake and filled with panic as she saw dead and wilting branches, peeling bark, charcoaled bodies, needles strewn on the ground, encircling the fragile trees like shadowed halos.

A page of the Great Story, Connie Barlow believes, is when we humans were born, and another was when we became aware of the flood we are causing.

Some scientists, however, believe the Guardians are a catastrophe. Famed biologist Daniel Simberloff has called assisted migration and Connie Barlow's work "ecological roulette." Jason McLachlan, a paleoecologist at Notre Dame, claims the Torreya Guardians' actions "will be a disaster" and that their logic is "pure bullshit."

These scientists are horrified by invasiveness, the idea of a foreigner running amok like kudzu or Asian carp or white Europeans. In their view, taking one animal, plant, or fungus out of a given environment and predicting its life in another is infeasible, a die cast.

But this fright escapes the notice of hordes of horticulturists and gardeners and farmers and ranchers. They've long grown foreign plants like soy and daikon and corn and potatoes, hybrid creatures like tangelos and Sun Gold tomatoes, European crossbreeds, Polynesian transplants, species from every corner of six continents. In any American ornamental garden anywhere there sprout foreign flower armies.

Paleobotany studies have revealed that early Americans gardened forests and plains; the Great Plains grass's adaptation to fire, for instance, was a human-forced one. And humans have moved species already because of climate change. More than 1,200 have been documented shifting habitat in the last thirty years.

It is not hubris anymore to say that people are at the helm of the planetary ship. There is no "leaving alone" when eight billion people crowd the Earth's skin.

Perhaps it is from a projected memory of blissful cohabitation that some scientists dig their boots in, resisting the recognition of our historical, global impact on worldkind. Perhaps they cannot see how the death of Eden will enable a new story.

The man who classified the stinking cedar was a Florida lawyer and botanist, Hardy Croom, who named the stinking tree after science colleague John Torrey.

In October 1837, Hardy Croom boarded a paddle steamer in New York with his wife and three children, heading for their domicile in the South. The vessel, with 133 people on board, was called Home. Off Cape Hatteras, the steamer encountered gale-force winds. Ocean spilled over the sides, and every passenger bailed with pans and pails, including Croom and his wife. When the sea snuffed out the engines, the boat drifted toward shore and hung up on the rocks. A survivor report told of Hardy Croom's youngest son gripping the rail of the steamship, watching his family slip, one by one, mother, father, siblings, into the sea, until he too, the little boy, was washed away.

Following the disaster, Congress enacted the Steamboat Act, requiring every vessel to carry a life vest for every passenger.

The waves that sank Croom and his family, that dragged him to the frigid depths from the pursuit of uncatalogued life, caused him, and the other ninety lost souls on board the Home, to have a lasting effect on our travels. Every time a person sees a traffic-cone-orange pile of flotation devices aboard a ferry, or feels the secure Styrofoam-like fluff beneath a water-borne seat, or is saved by one in an unexpected storm or a grounding or a too-tight turn, she should thank Hardy Croom, the first cataloguer of stinking cedars, and his wife and his innocent children and those that went down on the Home, for their deaths provided salvation to float upon.

Torreya State Park is soft and fertile with a tree canopy high and shady when I visit in July. There is a sense of the neo-tropical, a rest stop, I imagine, for Appalachia moisture on its way to the equator.

I am here to see the last stinking cedars. There are around two hundred in the park, 73 percent diseased and 60 percent antlered by whitetail deer. The rest are noodling toward the sky but dying young, like tales that can't quite grasp the imagination.

The torreyas I find first are locked inside steel mesh cages and, almost to a one, are as bare as sand-blasted marble. The stinking cedar remains are a dull brown, and each part appears shriveled, shrunken. All but three of the first trees I spot have lost their crown needles. They look like spent torches standing upright.

I toe the limp branch of a torreya, finger the dead crowns. It would be a sad thing, I think, to name a park after a tree that goes extinct.

Stinking cedars are also called gopher trees. But "gopher wood" has nothing to do with burrowing animals. It is an anachronistic moniker whose meaning is lost in time and translation.

Gopher trees would prove essential to the lifework of a Florida lawyer turned biblical explorer named Elvy Edison Callaway.

E. E. Callaway was sixty-five in 1945 when he sat in the office of a ninety-eight-year-old physician turned metaphysician, Dr. Brown Landone. The older man had spent his life with the Gnostic Order of Melchizedek and had written a number of spiritual texts, such as *Transforming Your Life in 24 Hours*.

Callaway was a lean and question-mark-shaped man, and Dr. Landone must have found him amicable and/or in search of meaning, for he gave the younger lawyer his Teleois Key, an algorithmic formula based on the numbers 1, 4, and 7.

The Teleois Key translated and transmitted knowledge of God. It told Landone to instruct Callaway to go to North Florida on a secret mission, on which he would not elaborate further.

The good doctor died two weeks later.

In an area, and an era, of rampant conservatism, Callaway was pro-civil-rights, pro-suffrage, pro-birth-control, anti-prohibition, and argued cases for the NAACP. Prior to meeting Landone, the decisive moment of Callaway's life might have been the meeting of his wife, a schoolteacher, at a square dance, an illicit date that led Callaway to be kicked out of his Baptist church.

It's unclear why Callaway would listen to Landone and his Dan Brown–esque eccentricities. Perhaps regrets about his marriage (which soon crumpled) or his family (which he soon abandoned), or his sense of the meaning of life, which for many is absent as they grow old, itched at him until he made the drive north from Tampa in 1953.

Callaway traveled to Bristol at the edge of the Florida Panhandle wilderness, where still two-thirds of the county was uninhabited. He examined the land near where modern-day Torreya State Park sits. He breathed in the mountain air that rolls off cliffs and collides with ocean. He kicked an Appalachian rock that had been scooted thousands of miles by ice.

He learned, he wrote later, that the best honey came from tupelo trees. The tastiest fruits grew in Florida soil. The best gold was found in its rock. The purest waters poured from the Smokey Mountains, nourishing the planet's most succulent oysters. And people in North Florida lived longer.

Callaway discovered that four rivers flowed into one, the wide, alligator-filled Apalachicola. Very rarely do four rivers trickle together. Nowhere, claimed Callaway, except the lost world of the Tigris, Euphrates, Gihon, and Pishon.

Then Callaway rediscovered what some people in North Florida still call gopher wood.

Soon he announced to the world that he had located the Garden of Eden in Bristol County, Florida.

The second day I am in Torreya State Park, my lemongrass insect repellent proves more of a dinner bell than a deterrent. From the moment I'm on trail looking for stinking cedars, I have twenty mosquitoes orbiting my face with the noise of squealing motors.

Golden orb weaver spiders dominate the trees. They are phosphorescent arachnids with leg spans as wide as coffee cans. When I don't face-plant their webs, I stir up their homes with a stick while their scurrying masses send phantom ice down my spine.

Meanwhile, ticks leap for my calves and chiggers burrow in my socks. Copperheads buzz nearby, and there's my fear of alligators at river's edge and black bears and Florida panthers.

Also, the crew of Animal Planet's *Finding Bigfoot* is filming in the park. However, I understand them as more Eden-getters, pursuing a missing link to a prophecy of our reacquaintance with a world lost.

I pick up a piece of cane with five leaves on it and begin slapping mosquitoes, my shoulders, face, ears, my skin goose-pimpling. I stare at the ground to spot snakes, conjure a hole in space with my stick to catch the orb weavers' nests, one foot in front of the other, singing Bob Dylan to alerts bears and maybe 'squatch too.

Add the blanketing humidity, and I have a hellacious experience searching for torreyas in the Garden of Eden.

Callaway wasn't the first to pursue the lost world. Columbus went prospecting for Eden in Venezuela. Dr. Livingstone presumed it was in Zambia. John Calvin preached that it lay hidden beneath Iraq. William Warren, president of Boston University, took a sabbatical and went on an Arctic cruise to confirm its location at the pole.

The Garden has been the illusory dream of scientists, kings, writers, and at least one southern lawyer. It is a story so compelling they've sometimes abandoned gold, tenure, country, and family.

I see it as reflecting a Puritan streak, a desire to get back to a mythical flawless existence. A natural heaven realized. As the thinking goes, we pulled stakes during Genesis or the Green Revolution or the Industrial. And if we could only find our way home, across time and evolution and technology, flip through the pages of the Great Story, we could be at peace with creation, as we were at mankind's introduction, before the plot became messy.

If only we could return to that treasured beginning that is not bound within the covers of any history.

After an hour of singing and slapping, I find a healthy torreya, a miniature tree about two and a half feet tall, wrapped in a cage. The torreya is finger-thin, but thriving, a darker hue than what I've seen earlier, zestier and lizard-skin green.

Besides climate change, deer, and parasites, the stinking cedars suffer their ancient root stock. The only torreyas around are old roots that sprout trunks, because the trees do not live long enough to seed. Eventually the stock will rot as will the young progeny, before they have time to seed out descendants.

It strikes me as an irony for the species itself, an ancient tree kept perpetually immature. Like a man-child absorbed in fantasy.

The stinking cedars do not seem at home amid all this aggression, crowded by gargantuan beech, ash, palm, and short leaf pine. They look shrunken, emaciated, out of place, everything else in Florida so robust and deadly.

It is only until the sixth torreya that I think so. The sixth tree is growing on a slope where stands of hickory and magnolia and needle palm encircle it.

At this torreya, all the mosquitoes stop whining, and sunbeams break the canopy. The biblical rays illumine a twenty-foot evergreen that smells like turpentine and mammalian sewage.

The tree appears as it should in its habitat—a mid-canopy species that is finally in mid-canopy. Not dwindled and crippled as its cousins crowded by hardwoods are, not meek or unneeded.

For the first time a stinking cedar appears to me to look at home, with a little bit of sun, but shaded by an ash, circled by palms. This torreya shines, the dew on its needles like gold coins.

The fantasy is that the stinking cedars will keep sprouting saplings from their decrepit root stock until one seeds. But it takes Samsonian efforts to keep the trees alive. The biologist at the state park described for me on the phone the hours required to cage the saplings against deer, burn away competition, and keep parasites at bay.

Many scientists claim, because of the variables, that what the Torreya Guardians are doing is setting an irresponsible precedent.

But Europeans began burning coal to manufacture steam in the eighteenth century, which germinated into climate change. Around the same time, they exported plants and animals along with capitalism.

More recently, the ten warmest years on record have occurred since 1998.

Considering the phrase "loss of innocence," Christopher Hitchens writes that "no other culture is so addicted to this narcissistic impression of itself as having any innocence to lose in the first place."

At Torreya State Park, I stand and take the trees in, amazed I am beholding a living ancient in its habitat, older than dinosaurs, rarer now in the world than diamonds.

I know that every molecule floats back into the river of time. We spiral out with the galaxies we're born from to one day end up suspended, cold in a lifeless but ever-expanding universe. The Great Story's great end.

But some deaths, like Hardy Croom's, can have redemption.

What I fear is the inability to know the largest scale on which every turn, every bon voyage leads to an unpredictable future. That we decide those futures now, with one seed in one hand and the other hand at the wheel.

But we've already cast anchor, which is as undeniable as the glacier melt haloing Greenland or the hundred species of tree frogs winking out in Costa Rica. Or the stinking cedars dying in their home.

I'm not sure when I realized that gopher wood, for Callaway, meant stinking cedars. According to Genesis, gopher wood is the tree Noah felled to construct his ark.

Noah squeezed out gopher sap for the boat's pitch. He sawed torreya lumber for the boat's keel and hull and decks. He then, goes the tale, loaded up two of every creature, waited for the rain, and floated for five months. The ship grounded on a mountain, and from there Noah descended to the cradle of civilization.

Humanity blossomed, its origins forgotten, the stinking cedar the lifeboat that rescued mankind.

There is something, for me, to Callaway's rediscovery of gopher wood in Florida, something about the weakest becoming salvation because they show us what is possible.

Which maybe means that after centuries of unconscious gardening and decimating, people could become an ark. That a mass extinction like us could possess the awareness that every volcano, asteroid, or sea boil has lacked. That maybe we aren't lost environmental sinners. But a death is necessary, and I feel that we must kill the idea that our innocence in the world was ever possible.

Extinctions are as ordinary as life. Molecules from ancient supernovas form our skins, our neurons, our thoughts, as do the cadavers of Triassic ferns.

But perhaps a conscious act can cut away illusions, free our evolutionary rudder. Perhaps this new myth discovered by Callaway helps us globe-trot into *Homo* truly *sapiens*.

We may ground on a mountain or capsize in a hurricane. But leaving port is the only possible plotline, because Eden, whatever it was, flooded in this story long ago.

If torreyas were gopher wood, the rare trees floored the pens of two of every living animal in the Genesis menagerie. The stinking trees creaked under horses' hooves, elephants rutting, tigers sharpening their claws, and snow monkeys urinating, which the stinking cedar would have absorbed without smelling much different.

I imagine the flood survivors standing watch on a deck made from torreyas, an olive-branch-bearing dove perching on a stinking rail. Torreya roof, torreya bow, torreya keel. The great oceanic assisted migration that carried life to our salvation made from gopher wood.

That we might be on the brink of taking a step toward accepting responsibility for this story fills me with cautious awe. People, the iceberg, the asteroid, the pyroclastic cloud, may yet carry something to the edge of the world on a rainbow promise.

The alternative myth, I suppose, is tragedy.

Callaway's new property was just south of what would become Torreya State Park. He transformed the land into a road-trip attraction. He painted large signs announcing the Garden of Eden to the highways. Tickets went on sale from a kiosk for $1.10. Callaway would refund your money if it rained or if you got lost coming down.

Visitors could drive into Callaway's theme park and climb the four-mile Garden of Eden Road. The entrance was a dirt path that rolled over plains, skirted a steep ravine, ascended through forest, and wrapped around sandy hills, flanked by wily tortoises and salamanders and Callaway's gopher trees.

Callaway dug up three petrified stinking cedar logs and set them on display. He claimed they were extras from the construction of the ark.

Elvy Callaway believed his mission from the Teleois Key was to bring Eden back to the world. To mark all the trees that signaled Noah's departure and share their message.

Inside his ramshackle tourist attraction, Callaway set out signs identifying landmarks. On one was lettered "Birth place of Adam." Another read "Ladies, on this natural operating table God took a rib from Adam's side and made mother Eve."

Another hand-painted marker read "The Leaves Of Gopher Trees is a perfect Design Conveying a Special Divine Message. No Other Tree in The World Has Such a Message."

Callaway's contrarian revision of the Fall, he wrote in one of his two memoirs, is that Eve knowingly chewed the apple.

She ate and got Adam to eat, not to be cast out of the Garden but to take responsibility for the lives that they were given. To lead them beyond innocence.

Epilogue
THE GENEALOGY OF EXTINCTION

THE CAMBRIAN

Not everything goes extinct. Sturgeon date back 200 million years, cockroaches 350 million. And cyanobacteria, photosynthesizing single-cell organisms, are 3 billion years old. But the universe's strings trend otherwise. Lately I've been thinking about the mass graves pockmarking our world, the six mass extinctions, including our own era's, that have altered life's composition. And as the weather responds and weirdens to climate change, the forest fires blazing, the eyes of hurricanes dotting the Atlantic, I wonder: what does it mean to be conductors of evolution?

But I am suspicious of guilt, I guess, because it's selfish and keeps me from looking inward in that it is post-trial, post-judgment. It harkens to a neo-Puritan fatalism, destructive because it presumes none of us can recover. I also wonder how much aberration there is in our human warring, stockpiling, nest-building, dam-making, colony-forming, traveling, rollicking, gazing curiosity. When I look at the geologic record, at mass extinctions, it seems like peeking into a mirror—not a resemblance to an ideal but a reflection of our own invasive species' dimensions in space and time.

I began caring about extinction when it was clear my conservative father wasn't going to recover from a lemon-sized brain tumor. Since he was a Rush Limbaugh acolyte, agnostic to the environment, I pushed away the parts of myself I found most similar to him. Realizing this now, I'm still grateful for the awareness I've gained, the knowledge of our continents' and oceans' dimming. Often something has to die so something else may evolve.

After witnessing his Los Alamos detonation, Robert Oppenheimer said he thought of the *Bhagavad Gita* line "Now I am become Death, the destroyer of worlds." What does it mean to become gods, not by right, but by happenstance, an inheritance of accumulated genetic material from, and onward to, an explosive moment? Can we take stock of our inheritance?

THE ORDOVICIAN

Before the first mass extinction, the Ordovician, the world was populated by giant sea scorpions, trilobites, reef-forming corals, and the first jawed fish. Then continent-sized glaciers sponged up the oceans, drying out our ancestors' homes.

One survivor from the Ordovician extinction was a teardrop-shaped arachnid with a harpoon tail. Closer to a lobster than a spider, the creature was armed with rigid plating and spindly legs that hugged the ground, letting it roll over the ocean floor like a crustacean tank. This was the horseshoe crab, still alive and now famous for its blue blood and medically revolutionary bio-coagulants. Likely few people reading these lines haven't benefited from a common inoculation using the milky blue mined from a horseshoe crab's heart. Its blood contains cells that bind to an inoculation's invasive contaminants like duct tape, rendering them inert.

The crabs are kidnapped from their homes for this, relieved of up to a third of their blood, and returned to the ocean. But lethargic after their blood donation, the crabs cannot swim the tides to spawn on shore, and their populations are dwindling.

The horseshoe crabs evolved their brilliant blue mechanism to survive five mass extinctions and all the diseases in between, but they are sapped for what has kept them alive for so long.

Sometimes this is true in the human world as well, that what once helped a person is later a death sentence. You can do a job well, for instance, as my own father did at a Corpus Christi bank where he rose from clerk to vice president. When I was growing up, he had a commanding corner office in a six-story building and drove a Lincoln Town Car. But his boss, the bank president, was laundering money for the last remnants of the Texas Mafia in the 1980s. And when he was caught, he brought the bank down. One of my dad's friends and business partners washed up on shore, a three-day-old ballooning corpse that made the cover of *Texas Monthly*. Dad, as a confederate, was dragged into the investigations and lawsuits. I doubt he reaped any of the Mafia's kickback, but I believe he looked the other way when hands slid under the table. His name tarnished, he found the same financial work impossible.

Dad gained weight while applying for jobs, and he watched hours and hours of sports. Before, we had taken the Lincoln on skiing vacations. Then he job-searched for three years, and we lost our home. The Lincoln rusted. By the time I was in fifth grade, my brother and I were eating free school lunches.

THE DEVONIAN

Just before the Devonian mass extinction, the ocean life's land assault had begun. Plants marched up the beach, then marshes evolved, then freshwater fish and amphibians. They surfaced, took a gulp, and then, lifetimes later, a breath. The Devonian rivers teemed, populated with froglike hybrids sunning themselves on ferns as thick as trees.

Life was crowded in the seas, food scarce, predators plentiful. This was why sea creatures escaped to land. And this was why, eons later, whales slipped back into the ocean, a vestige of their suburban flight visible in tiny, useless feet.

Thinking about this makes me realize the world is not a stable tapestry but a kaleidoscope of creatures eager for existence, flux the only constant in the pouring of biology across time zones and continents. And I say this subjectively, because I think ecology is subjective. I find it appealing to look at the Earth and ask what it wants and find "survival"—liberating, as no other species has the angst I do about finding meaning in the rock table.

———

Now I'm trying to unpack my family history as it relates to geology, sandstone layers bleeding into shale as my dad feeds into me. But it's difficult to see myself in time's arrow or jumble of moments congealed into stone. A plesiosaur can't leave the rock table and examine its clayed fin prints.

In the Devonian, coral systems grew twice as large as the Great Barrier Reef. They harbored underwater forests of sea lilies resembling gaunt women with hair caught in a turbulent breeze. Early giant squids inked, and tulip-shaped flowers bloomed, and many varieties of brachiopod shellfish colored the sandy shores. You could not have strolled a beach without your toes curling around the rainbow-shelled Devonian menagerie.

For reasons that aren't understood, the reefs collapsed. As did the brachiopods and the squids and the tentaculitids, these last a strand of plankton that lined the ocean surface in countless quintillions. They lay on the seafloor as they died, their sheer mass compressing itself into limestone, in which fully formed fossils can still be found.

They are memories within a memory.

When an extinction leaves a niche (tentaculitids', for instance), another creature fills it (such as plankton). My mother knows this from calling Dad's office at an oil company where he worked for one year after the bank's demise. When the oil funding dried up like so many of the wells in Texas, he was fired but kept the truth hidden. Until another man picked up his line.

What was my father doing for six months, jobless? I think it was much like the time when, years later, he held on to the hope that his life could be restored, even after the cancer detonated in his brain. He would say then, "If I just could get another chance," and repeat this like a koan.

He thought if he withheld the truth from my mother, his world would go back to spinning the way it was. But who can unflood the glacier-melt oceans? Or give back the Mafia's money once it's been cleaned? Who can stop up the Earth's volcanoes when they hiccup their warmth?

THE GREAT DYING

To picture the third mass extinction, the Permian, known as the Great Dying, it's good to recall the lava bubble that rose to the surface of Lake Nyos in Cameroon in 1986. Carbon dioxide locked in the crust under Africa was churned by tectonics and floated to the surface, bursting like soda fizz. The air killed hundreds of Cameroonians and their livestock sleeping along the cool shore.

This was like the Permian extinction, only then the lethal bubbles covered an ocean. At the same time, the Earth witnessed its greatest volcanic eruption. Basalt lifted from under Siberia and covered a Europe-sized patch of Asia. Flaming lava piled four miles into the sky.

Combined, the events melted frozen bogs, triggered acid rain, and swathed the globe in a sulfur dioxide fog. The event was so intense that early twentieth-century scientists theorized that a supernova had blanketed the Earth: a galaxy-sized atomic bomb.

This is similar to our human-induced extinction, as we pump fossil fuels into our world's troposphere where it traps the fireflies of the sun's rays. Upwards of 75 percent of the planet may wink out by the end of the century, and who knows how many will die later on.

THE CRETACEOUS

When my father stayed home after the oil company withered, effectively jobless, it had been a joyful thing for me to have him around, to be able to fossilize greater fragments of him in my memory. We played football, we ate 49-cent hot dogs at Wienerschnitzel, and I think my mother was jealous even of the time we spent, a seed that caused her sudden, flaring outbursts of anger. It was she, after all, who took care of our survival, working two jobs as a teacher and as a researcher. My father was content, it seemed, to let his pigskin missiles sail into the blinding light of noon and watch the shadows fall over this boy's face as the leather egg landed in my arms.

Sometimes you can see extinction coming, like my parent's divorce.

And had you stood beneath the Chicxulub meteor, you would have witnessed the atmosphere opening behind a debris trail, revealing the blue-black of space and stars. They shimmered on the horizon during the bright light of day.

For a second, that is, until everything around vaporized. Any unlucky creature's atoms were carried away with an ice cream scoop of earth to the far reaches of the world and perhaps littering the moon and Mars.

Dinosaurs now mean more to many children than do living animals. Like other six-year-old arms, mine once cradled the plastic replicas of brachiosaurus and parasaurolophus, those composites of petroleum congealed from festering long-ago ferns. My playthings were these creatures' breakfasts before they died, our lives as interconnected as the world extending backward in time.

Dinos and our ancestor mammals arose simultaneously around 200 million years ago. As siblings, they diverged. One grew dominant, and the other lived in its shadow where many vulnerable things can develop. And then a gunshot from space, and the bigger sibling fell. The weaklings swelled to mastodons, tigers, orangutans, and galloping herds that recolonized the waters as whales and took to the air as bats.

So too will industrious flora and fauna reign during the twilight of Homo sapiens. Maybe we will see flying raccoons, mathematically inclined puffer fish, muscle-clad cockroaches. Survivors will radiate into unpredictable, mesmerizing forms.

The world is doomed only when the last flickering creature crumbles to dust, uneaten by extinct bacteria. Life, of course, rises from the dead's ashes.

It took my father eleven years to die. First the lemon-sized tumor. Then the legal limit for radiation treatments that fractured the capillaries in his skull. Four strokes, and hard-to-count mini ruptures. A slow withering march to extinction.

How much is enough life? Will I be happy at fifty-nine, the age my father learned of his cancer? Will I be satisfied with a world of ten million species or a hundred thousand?

No, I want as much life as possible, and there is no scientific argument here. I saw what not enough living did to my dad. I see what his and my generation have to cope with ecologically. I see the world they've handed down to us. When dealing with oblivion, I'm as greedy as they come.

THE ANTHROPOCENE

Humans have come close to extinction's razor. Not just the Black Plague but the flu of 1918, which originated in Asia and poured through Europe because of the Great War. It crossed the Atlantic and invaded even Eskimo villages and Pacific atolls. Half of the world was infected, and one in twenty of those perished.

One of the first writers to imagine a liquidation of human life was Mary Shelley. In 1826, several years after she created her immortal monster, and after her husband, Percy Shelley, drowned in the Mediterranean, she penned the novel *The Last Man*. The story follows a cohort of artsy heroes who resemble Percy and Lord Byron and their friends. They strive bravely and escape unlikely scenarios as pestilence envelopes Europe. Gradually in *The Last Man* all succumb until just three characters remain: a teenage girl, Percy Shelly's fictional stand-in, and the narrator, who is a widower. The girl and Percy, it is presumed, will marry and repopulate the planet. But after surviving all manner of near deaths, the pair drown, as Percy did. Only the narrator, an isolated scribe like Mary herself, is left to explore the emptied world. The narrator leaves behind a memoir in a cave for anyone who should find it: a story of extinction, written by a novelist who had lost the person orienting her life.

So it is with oblivion. The globe limps on, and old lives wink out. There is the trauma of letting go, of cradling loss. The cave is an apt metaphor, for it is a wound buried in living time. Caves appear in limestone, the rock made from fossilized bodies. Dripping water surgically opens caverns in those pulverized and pressurized leaves and bones of countless past lives. We crawl inside to see who we once were.

Will our species live on? Will my family? I have no child, but I wonder if occupying this niche, filling my dad's place, will ensure my offspring's survival should I have one. And by that I don't mean a pulse, I mean an existence enmeshed in the knowledge of things, a life engrossed by the world, ever searching.

But if a meteor crashed or my bowels should erupt with tumors, how would my progeny respond except to calculate how to survive what took me? I don't know how to proceed except to tell my story, my family's and the world's as entwined as helixes of DNA. The full picture, the jumbled song, the cosmic creation myth of our lives in rock as told through ascendants and departures. My child will have to read the fossilized footprints and decide where they lead.

Acknowledgments

Lots of thanks to Kim Cross for giving the book its title. To Tom Huang, who made me realize what the book is really about. To Kristen Radtke for all her book advice, and to Jericho Parms, Stephanie Elizondo Griest, Yelizaveta Renfro, Maggie Messitt, Lucas Mann, Toni Jensen, Elena Passarello, and Inara Verzemnieks for theirs too. To George Getschow, who does so much for his fellow writers, and who was kind enough to lend me his cockroach-in-the-ear story. Also to Lyz Lenz, Scott Gast, and Emily Nemens for being such great editors.

A big thanks to Beth Snead at the University of Georgia Press for seeing something worthwhile in this book. To B. K. Loren, Nicole Walker, and Ann Marlowe for their insightful and prodigious feedback.

Connie Barlow at the Torreya Guardians was very open to talking about the stinking cedar and even reading an early draft of the book. Jason McLachlan at the University of Notre Dame kindly spent time giving me his thoughts on invasive species. Jessica Hellmann at the University of Minnesota helped me understand how species react to climate change. And George Malanson at the University of Iowa introduced me to rabbits in Australia, from which this whole book spilled forth. Thank you, all.

I have a lot of mentors to thank, but few people have done as much to make me feel at home in the writing world as Jill Talbot; thank you for being a gracious colleague/mentor. And thank you to Kurt Caswell who always treated me like a colleague even when I clearly wasn't. Also, Robin Hemley was most patient when I came to Iowa for my MFA and was completely out of my league. Finally, Priscilla Ybarra, Dahlia Porter, and Barbara Eckstein challenged the ways I thought about environmental writing, and it's no hyperbole that this book wouldn't exist without them.

Thanks to my friends and partners in writing crime, who read and/or helped with earlier draftis: Kim Gaza, Amanda Kanowski, Charlie Riccardelli, Spencer Hyde, Ryan Flanagan, Zach Vande-Zande, A. Kendra Greene, Sarah Viren, Emily Ha, Bernice Santiago, and Angela Pelster-Wiebe. A huge thanks to Jenny Molberg and Phong Nguyen for believing I could help edit the lovely *Pleiades*.

I gratefully acknowledge the literary journals and sites that previously published, in slightly different form, the essays in this book:

"Seagulled" in *Orion*
"The Miracle Vine" in *The Awl*
"Rabbits and Convicts" in *North American Review*
"Beasts in the Street" in *Orion*
"Wildlife of Unknown Status" in *The Rumpus*
"The Texas Snow Monkeys" in *Columbia Journal*
"Uncle Shark" in *Upstreet*
"The Limbic System Roundup" in *The Rumpus*
"Becoming Mascot" in *Iron Horse Literary Review*
"Water Bugs: A Story of Absolution" in *Southern Review*
"A Passage of Birds" in *Lake Effect*
"The Color of Tarsiers" in *Cahoodaloodaling*
"The Carp Experience" in *DIAGRAM*
"Evolving the Monster: A History of Godzilla" in *Catapult*
"The Great Story of the Stinking Cedar in the Garden of Eden"
    in *Southwest Review*.

Thanks to my family.
And thanks to Yumiko, for where would I be without you?

Sources

PROLOGUE: SEAGULLED

National Park Service. "Padre Island National Seashore, Texas." www.nps
.gov/pais/index.

THE MIRACLE VINE

Alderman, Derek H. "Channing Cope and the Making of a Miracle Vine."
Geographical Review 94, no. 2 (2004): 157–77.
———. "Kudzu: A Tale of Two Vines." *Southern Cultures* 7, no. 3 (2001):
49–64.
Cope, Channing. *Front Porch Farmer*. Atlanta: T. E. Smith, 1949.
Dickey, James. "Kudzu." *New Yorker*, 18 May 1963. www.newyorker.com
/magazine/1963/05/18/kudzu.
Finch, Bill. "The True Story of Kudzu, the Vine That Never Truly Ate the
South." *Smithsonian*, September 2015. www.smithsonianmag.com
/science-nature/true-story-kudzu-vine-ate-south-180956325.
Hinman, Kristen. "Kudzu." *American History* 46, no. 2 (2011): 38–45.
Silvertown, Jonathan W. *Demons in Eden*. Chicago: University of Chicago
Press, 2005.
Stewart, Doug. "Kudzu: Love It—or Run." *Smithsonian*, October 2000.
www.smithsonianmag.com/science-nature/kudzu-love-it-or-run
-68095358.
Time. "The Kudzu Kid." 4 July 1949, 50–51.
U.S. Department of Agriculture, National Agricultural Library, National
Invasive Species Information Center. "Plants: Species Profiles: Kudzu."
www.invasivespeciesinfo.gov/plants/kudzu.shtml.
U.S. Department of Agriculture, Natural Resources Conservation Service.
"Plant Guide: Spanish Moss." plants.usda.gov/plantguide/pdf/cs_tius
.pdf.

University of Delaware Library, Special Collections Department. "The Centennial Exposition, Philadelphia, 1876." In *Progress Made Visible: American World's Fairs and Expositions*, curated by Iris R. Snyder, February 8–June 8, 2000. www.lib.udel.edu/ud/spec/exhibits/fairs/cent.htm.

RABBITS AND CONVICTS

Australian Government, Department of Agriculture and Water Resources. "A Statement from the Chief Veterinary Officer (Australia) on Myxomatosis Vaccine Availability in Australia." 2013. www.agriculture.gov.au /animal/health/myxomatosis-vaccine.

Bentham, Jeremy. "Panopticon versus New South Wales." In *The Works of Jeremy Bentham*, 4:173–211. Edinburgh: William Tait, 1838.

Bolton, Geoffrey. *Spoils and Spoilers: Australians Make Their Environment, 1788–1980.* Sydney: Allen and Unwin, 1981.

Burke, Edmund. *Reflections on the Revolution in France.* London: J. Dodsley, 1790.

Commonwealth Scientific and Industrial Research Organisation. "Myxomatosis to Control Rabbits." CSIROpedia, 2015. csiropedia.csiro.au /myxomatosis-to-control-rabbits.

Costello, Con. *Botany Bay: The Story of the Convicts Transported from Ireland to Australia, 1791–1853.* Cork: Mercier Press, 1987.

Dovers, Stephen, ed. *Australian Environmental History: Essays and Cases.* Melbourne: Oxford University Press, 1994.

———. "Still Discovering Monaro: Perceptions of Landscape." In Dovers, *Australian Environmental History,* 119–40.

Fry, Kenneth. "Kiola: A History of the Environmental Impact of European Occupation, 1830–1980." In Dovers, *Australian Environmental History,* 99–118.

Government of Western Australia, Department of Primary Industries and Regional Development: Agriculture and Food. "Rabbit Control Options." www.agric.wa.gov.au/baits-poisons/rabbit-control-options.

Green, Michael. "Once Were Warriors." *Sydney Morning Herald,* 5 February 2014. www.smh.com.au/national/once-were-warriors -20140204-31zmu.html.

Hughes, Robert. *The Fatal Shore.* New York: Knopf, 1987.

Morton, Stephen. "European Settlement and the Mammals of Arid Australia." In Dovers, *Australian Environmental History,* 141–66.

National Library of Australia. "The State Barrier Fence of Western Australia: Centenary, 1901–2001." pandora.nla.gov.au/pan/43156/20040709 -0000/agspsrv34.agric.wa.gov.au/programs/app/barrier/history.htm.

Pfeffer, Jeremy I. *From One End of the Earth to the Other: The London Bet Din, 1805–1855, and the Jewish Convicts Transported to Australia*. Brighton: Sussex Academic Press, 2008.

Pybus, Cassandra, and Hamish Maxwell-Stewart. *American Citizens, British Slaves: Yankee Political Prisoners in an Australian Penal Colony, 1839–1850*. East Lansing: Michigan State University Press, 2002.

Ricciardi, Anthony, and Daniel Simberloff. "Assisted Colonization Is Not a Viable Conservation Strategy." *Trends in Ecology and Evolution* 24, no. 5 (2009): 248–53.

Rolls, Eric. "More a New Planet Than a New Continent." In Dovers, *Australian Environmental History*, 22–33.

Sharp, Trudy, and Glen Saunders. "Rabbit Warren Destruction by Ripping." New South Wales Department of Primary Industries, 10 January 2004. www.pestsmart.org.au/wp-content/uploads/2012/05/RAB006.pdf.

Shelley, Percy Bysshe. "Peter Bell the Third." In *Shelley's Poetry and Prose*, edited by Neil Fraistat and Donald H. Reiman. New York: Norton, 2002.

Tan, Shaun, and John Marsden. "The Rabbits." In *Lost and Found: Three by Shaun Tan*. New York: Scholastic, Arthur A. Levine Books, 2011.

BEASTS ON THE STREET

Centers for Disease Control and Prevention. "Pedestrian Safety." www.cdc.gov/motorvehiclesafety/pedestrian_safety.

Guinness World Records. "First Person Killed by a Car." www.guinnessworldrecords.com/world-records/first-person-killed-by-a-car.

Herrel, Katie. "Ask a Bear: How Many Bear Attacks, Really?" *Backpacker*, 1 December 2009. www.backpacker.com/news-and-events/news/trail-news/ask-a-bear-how-many-bear-attacks-really-2.

Loomis, Bill. "1900–1930: The Years of Driving Dangerously." *Detroit News*, 26 April 2015. www.detroitnews.com/story/news/local/michigan-history/2015/04/26/auto-traffic-history-detroit/26312107.

McFarlane, Andrew. "How the UK's First Fatal Car Accident Unfolded." *BBC News*, 17 August 2010. www.bbc.com/news/magazine-10987606.

Quammen, David. *Monster of God: The Man-Eating Predator in the Jungles of History and the Mind*. New York: Norton, 2003.

Thompson, Clive. "When Pedestrians Ruled the Road." *Smithsonian*, December 2015. www.smithsonianmag.com/innovation/when-pedestrians-ruled-streets-180953396.

WILDLIFE OF UNKNOWN STATUS

Baron, David. *The Beast in the Garden: A Modern Parable of Man and Nature.*
New York: Norton, 2004.

Beier, Paul, and Andrew J. Gregory. "Desperately Seeking Stable 50-Year-
Old Landscapes with Patches and Long, Wide Corridors." PLoS Biology
10, no. 1 (2012). journals.plos.org/plosbiology/article?id=10.1371
/journal.pbio.1001253.

Flores, Dan. *Coyote America: A Natural and Supernatural History.* New York:
Basic Books, 2016. (Goldman quote on 123.)

Florida Wildlife Corridor website. floridawildlifecorridor.org.

Frost, Robert. "A Servant to Servants." In *Collected Poems of Robert Frost,*
82–87. New York: Henry Holt, 1930.

Hiss, Tony. "Can the World Really Set Aside Half of the Planet for Wildlife?" *Smithsonian,* September 2014, 67–78. www.smithsonianmag
.com/science-nature/can-world-really-set-aside-half-planet-wildlife
-180952379.

Jones, Mike. Personal interview, 17 July 2012.

Karsai, Istvan, and George Kampis. "Connected Fragmented Habitats
Facilitate Stable Coexistence Dynamics." *Ecological Modeling* 222 (2011):
447–55.

Lallanilla, Marc. "Why Sinkholes Are Eating Florida." *Yahoo! News,* 6 March
2013. www.yahoo.com/news/why-sinkholes-eating-florida-150755319
.html?ref=gs.

Maehr, David S. *The Florida Panther: Life and Death of a Vanishing Carnivore.*
Washington, D.C.: Island Press, 1997.

Metcalf, Franz. *What Would Buddha Do? 101 Answers to Life's Daily Dilemmas.*
Berkeley, Cal.: Ulysses Press, 1999. (Shinran quote on 124.)

Pearce, Fred. "Corridors of Uncertainty." *New Scientist* 213, no. 2850 (2012):
26–27.

Tallahassee Museum website. tallahasseemuseum.org.

Thatcher, Cindy, Frank T. van Manen, and Joseph D. Clark. "Identifying
Suitable Sites for Florida Panther Reintroduction." *Journal of Wildlife
Management* 70, no. 3 (2006): 752–63.

U.S. Fish and Wildlife Service. "Florida Panther." www.fws.gov/refuge
/florida_panther.

White, Mel. "Path of the Jaguars." *National Geographic,* March 2009. http://
archive.is/OUcY.

THE TEXAS SNOW MONKEYS

Ajax, Tim (director, Born Free USA Primate Sanctuary). Personal interview,
3 March 2012.

Baker, Ed. "The Legendary Snow Monkeys of Texas." *Austin Chronicle*, 5 August 2005. www.austinchronicle.com/news/2005-08-05/283057.

Bauman, Zygmunt. *Globalization: The Human Consequences*. New York: Columbia University Press, 1998.

Born Free USA. "Primate Sanctuary." www.bornfreeusa.org/sanctuary.

Derrida, Jacques. *The Animal That Therefore I Am*. Translated by David Wills. New York: Fordham University Press, 2008.

de Waal, Frans. *The Ape and the Sushi Master: Cultural Reflections of a Primatologist*. New York: Basic Books, 2001.

Emlen, John. Foreword to Fedigan and Asquith, *The Monkeys of Arashiyama*, xii–xv.

Fedigan, Linda Marie. "History of the Arashiyama West Japanese Macaques in Texas." In Fedigan and Asquith, *The Monkeys of Arashiyama*, 54–73.

Fedigan, Linda Marie, and Pamela J. Asquith, eds. *The Monkeys of Arashiyama*. Albany: State University of New York Press, 1991.

Haraway, Donna J. *When Species Meet*. Minneapolis: University of Minnesota Press, 2008.

Huffman, Michael A. "History of the Arashiyama Macaques in Kyoto, Japan." In Fedigan and Asquith, *The Monkeys of Arashiyama*, 21–53.
————. Personal interview, 14 April 2014.

Huffman, Michael A., et al. "A Brief Historical Timeline of Research on the Arashiyama Macaques." In Leca, Huffman, and Vasey, *Monkeys of Stormy Mountain*, 13–27.

Leca, Jean-Baptiste, Michael A. Huffman, and Paul L. Vasey, eds. *The Monkeys of Stormy Mountain: 60 Years of Primatological Research on the Japanese Macaques of Arashiyama*. Cambridge: Cambridge University Press, 2012.

Ohta, Eiji. "In Search of the Phantom Monkeys." Translated by Michael A. Huffman. In Leca, Huffman, and Vasey, *Monkeys of Stormy Mountain*, 28–33.

Reeves, Jim. "Nolan Ryan Knows All about (Snow) Monkey Business." *Fort Worth Star Telegram*, 1 July 2012. www.star-telegram.com/sports/article3831863.html.

Sugiyama, Yukimaru. "Arashiyama Monkeys in the Late 1950s." In Leca, Huffman, and Vasey, *Monkeys of Stormy Mountain*, 34–44.

TheUnTicket.com. "Nolan Ryan Talks About Snow Monkeys." 3 December 2008. www.theunticket.com/nolan-ryan-talks-about-snow-monkeys.

Thierry, Bernard, et al. "Why Macaque Societies?" In *Macaque Societies: A Model for the Study of Social Organization*, edited by Bernard Thierry, Mewa

Singh, and Werner Kaumanns, 3–10. Cambridge: Cambridge University Press, 2004.

THE LIMBIC SYSTEM ROUNDUP

Armstrong, Terry (Sweetwater Jaycees). Personal interview, 13 March 2015.

Boundless. "The Limbic System." www.boundless.com/psychology
/textbooks/boundless-psychology-textbook/biological-foundations-of
-psychology-3/structure-and-function-of-the-brain-35/the-limbic
-system-154-12689. Accessed 28 December 2016.

Dahlitz, Matthew. "The Limbic System." Neuropsychotherapist, 27 December 2016. www.neuropsychotherapist.com/the-limbic-system.

Dart, Tom. "Snakes on the Plain: Texas Festival Sees Pageant Winners Wade through Rattler Pit." Guardian, 14 March 2015. www.theguardian
.com/us-news/2015/mar/14/snakes-on-the-plain-texas-festival-sees
-pageant-winners-wade-through-rattler-pit.

Hazlitt, William. "On the Pleasure of Hating." 1826. In The Art of the Personal Essay, edited by Phillip Lopate, 189–97. New York: Anchor, 1994.

National Geographic. "Rattlesnake Roundup." American Festivals Project video, 2010. video.nationalgeographic.com/video/american-festivals
-project/rattlesnake-roundup.

Rubio, Manny. Rattlesnake: Portrait of a Predator. Washington, D.C.: Smithsonian Institution Press, 1998.

Smith, Amber. "Threats to Biodiversity through Current Rattlesnake Roundup Practices." Master's thesis, Miami University, 2015.

Sweetwater Jaycees. "World's Largest Rattlesnake Roundup." www
.rattlesnakeroundup.net.

Townsend, Wendy. "'Rattlesnake Roundup' Teaches Cruelty Is Fun." CNN, 9 April 2014. www.cnn.com/2014/04/09/opinion/townsend
-rattlesnake-roundup.

Werler, John E., and James R. Dixon. Texas Snakes: Identification, Distribution, and Natural History. Austin: University of Texas Press, 2000.

BECOMING MASCOT

Abram, David. The Spell of the Sensuous: Perception and Language in a More-Than-Human World. New York: Pantheon, 1996.

Associated Press. "Rebel Black Bear Is Ole Miss Mascot." 14 October 2010. www.espn.com/college-sports/news/story?id=5684400.

Baranko, Jessica. "Hear Me Roar: Should Universities Use Live Animals As Mascots?" Marquette Sports Law Review 21, no. 2 (2011). scholarship.law
.marquette.edu/cgi/viewcontent.cgi?article=1534&context=sportslaw.

Campus Explorer. "Top 10 Weirdest Mascots." www.campusexplorer.com
    /Top-10-Weirdest-College-Mascots.
Lee, Amber. "Strangest Mascot Injuries." Bleacher Report, 3 December 2013.
    bleacherreport.com/articles/1874897-strangest-mascot-injuries.
Texas Tech Spirit Program. "Texas Tech Masked Rider Program History."
    www.depts.ttu.edu/centerforcampuslife/spiritsquads/MR_history
    .php.
Tracy, Marc. "In Death, As in Life, It's Royal Treatment for Animal Mas-
    cots." New York Times, 4 April 2015. www.nytimes.com/2015/04/05
    /sports/ncaabasketball/in-death-as-in-life-its-royal-treatment-for
    -animal-mascots.html.
Tufts University. "Jumbo the Mascot." www.tufts.edu/about/jumbo.
Twist NHook. "Inside the Phoenix Five." SB Nation: California Golden
    Blogs, 8 July 2008. www.californiagoldenblogs.com/2008/7/9/564303
    /inside-the-phoenix-five.
University of California, Santa Cruz. "Banana Slug Mascot." www.ucsc
    .edu/about/mascot.html.
USA Today. "List of Schools That Changed Native American Nicknames."
    24 September 2013. www.usatoday.com/story/sports/2013/09/12
    /native-american-mascot-changes-ncaa/2804337.
Weber, Jim. "Nostalgia: When Bevo was Barbecue, and Other Trials of
    Texas' Most Famous Longhorn." Yahoo Sports, 24 November 2010.
    sports.yahoo.com/ncaa/football/blog/dr_saturday/post/Nostalgia
    -When-Bevo-was-barbecue-and-other-tri?urn=ncaaf-289081.

WATER BUGS: A STORY OF ABSOLUTION

Biehler, Dawn Day. Pests in the City: Flies, Bedbugs, Cockroaches, and Rats.
    Seattle: University of Washington Press, 2013.
Chalmers, Catherine. American Cockroach. New York: Aperture, 2004.
CNN. "Roach-Eating Contest Winner Choked to Death." 26 November
    2012. www.cnn.com/2012/11/26/us/florida-roach-eating-death/index
    .html.
Fox, Douglas. "Consciousness in a Cockroach." Discover, 10 January 2007.
    discovermagazine.com/2007/jan/cockroach-consciousness-neuron
    -similarity.
Getschow, George. Personal interview, 4 April 2016.
Kafka, Franz. Metamorphosis. Translated by A. L. Lloyd. New York: Van-
    guard, 1946.
Haraway, Donna. "Tunneling the Chthulucene." Keynote address, Associ-
    ation for the Study of Literature and the Environment Biannual Confer-

ence, University of Idaho, Moscow, Idaho, 25 June 2015. www.youtube
.com/watch?v=FkZSh8Wb-t8.

Hazlitt, William. "On the Pleasure of Hating." 1826. In *The Art of the Personal Essay*, edited by Phillip Lopate, 189–97. New York: Anchor, 1994.

Lockwood, Jeffrey A. *The Infested Mind: Why Humans Fear, Loathe, and Love Insects*. Oxford: Oxford University Press, 2013.

NBC News. "Florida Man Who Died in Cockroach-Eating Contest Choked to Death, Autopsy Says." 26 November 2012. usnews.newsvine.com /_news/2012/11/26/15460502-florida-man-who-died-in-cockroach -eating-contest-choked-to-death-autopsy-says?lite.

Nuwer, Rachel. "Cockroaches: The Insect We're Programmed to Fear." *BBC Future*, 18 September 2014. www.bbc.com/future/story/20140918 -the-reality-about-roaches.

O'Connell, Oliver. "Mother Charged after Her Dead Daughter Is Discovered Being Eaten by Cockroaches 'after She Abandoned Her on the Floor of Their Infested Apartment.'" *Daily Mail*, 20 April 2015. www .dailymail.co.uk/news/article-3048181/Mom-charged-child-neglect -baby-dead-covered-roach-bites-floor-infested-apartment.html.

Roadside America. "Plano, Texas: Cockroach Hall of Fame (Gone)." www .roadsideamerica.com/tip/1252.

Robinson, David. "The Bugs That Bugged the Colonists." *Colonial Williamsburg Journal*, Autumn 2007. www.history.org/Foundation/journal /Autumn07/bugs.cfm.

RT News. "Robo-Roach: Remote-Controlled Cockroaches at the Touch of a Button." 4 March 2015. www.rt.com/news/237605-cockroaches-rescue -robot-computer.

Rowley, Storer. "What's the Biggest Thing in Texas? Cockroaches, Y'all." *Chicago Tribune*, 17 July 1986. articles.chicagotribune.com/1986-07-17 /news/8602200749_1_texans-contest-houston.

Schweid, Richard. *The Cockroach Papers: A Compendium of History and Lore*. New York: Basic Books, 1999.

Sherk, Bill. *500 Years of New Words: The Fascinating Story of How, When, and Why These Words First Entered the English Language*. Rev. ed. Toronto: Dundurn, 2004.

Silverman, Lauren. "How The Biggest Cockroach in Dallas Made Michael Bohdan Famous." *KERA News*, 26 October 2016. keranews.org/post /how-biggest-cockroach-dallas-made-michael-bohdan-famous.

Sleigh, Charlotte. "Inside Out: The Unsettling Nature of Insects." In *Insect Poetics*, edited by Eric C. Brown, 281–97. Minneapolis: University of Minnesota Press, 2006.

Smith, John. *The Generall Historie of Virginia, New-England, and the Summer Isles*. London: Michael Sparkes, 1624.

Thompson, Paul. "Parents Facing Neglect Charges after Nine-Year-Old Son Found with a Cockroach in His Ear." *Daily Mail*, 15 February 2013. www.dailymail.co.uk/news/article-2279367/Parents-charged-neglect -year-old-son-cockroach-ear.html.

University of California Agriculture and Natural Resources. "Pests of Homes, Structures, People, and Pets." ipm.ucanr.edu/PMG /PESTNOTES/pn7467.html.

Williams, Zoe. "Katie Hopkins Calling Migrants Vermin Recalls the Darkest Events of History." *Guardian*, 19 April 2015. www.theguardian.com /commentisfree/2015/apr/19/katie-hopkins-migrants-vermin-darkest -history-drownings.

THE CARP EXPERIENCE

ABC News. "Carp, It's What's for Dinner?" 22 September 2011. abc7news .com/archive/8364300.

Abramajtys, Joe. "Asian Carp Frenzy: The Immigrant Experience." *Wake: Great Lakes Thoughts and Culture* 1, no. 2 (2012): 26–34.

———. "Carp & Dogs & Ponies: Government Plans Feature Lots of Show, Little Action." *Wake*, 13 September 2011. wakegreatlakes.org/content /nonfiction/asian-carp-frenzy-government-plans-lack-action. Accessed 31 December 2016.

American Public Works Association. "The Reversal of the Chicago River." www.apwa.net/about/awards/toptencentury/chica.htm.

American Society of Civil Engineers. "Top 10 Achievements & Millennium Monuments: Wastewater Treatment: Monument: Chicago Wastewater System." www.ktu.edu.tr/dosyalar/14_01_00_2d9a6.pdf.

Baichwal, Ravi. "Crews Shock Fish to Fight Asian carp." *ABC News*, 2 December 2009. abc7chicago.com/archive/7149369.

Barnes, Robert. "More Supreme Court Actions." *Washington Post*, 20 January 2010. www.washingtonpost.com/wp-dyn/content/article/2010/01 /19/AR2010011903955.

Belkin, Douglas. "Asian Carp Could Hurt Boating, Fishing Industry in Great Lakes." *Wall Street Journal*, 20 November 2009. www.wsj.com /articles/SB125874214275057775.

Dickinson, Meg. "Groups Say Asian Carp Could Help Solve Hunger in Illinois." *Champaign (Illinois) News-Gazette*, 28 June 2012. www.news-gazette .com/news/local/2012-06-28/groups-say-asian-carp-could-help-solve -hunger-illinois.html.

Eagan, Dan. "Fish Barrier vs. Carp DNA: What to Believe?" *Milwaukee Journal Sentinel*, 25 August 2012. archive.jsonline.com/news/wisconsin/fish-barrier-vs-carp-dna-what-to-believe-4q5ru75-167454795.html.

Encyclopedia Britannica. "Chicago Sanitary and Ship Canal." 29 January 2010. www.britannica.com/topic/Chicago-Sanitary-and-Ship-Canal.

Garcia, John. "One Asian Carp Found in Canal after Fish Kill." *ABC News*, 7 December 2009. abc7chicago.com/archive/7151833.

Hannah, Lee, ed. *Saving a Million Species: Extinction Risk from Climate Change*. Washington, D.C.: Island Press, 2012.

Hood, Joel, and James Janega. "Fight to Keep Asian Carp out of Great Lakes Reaches Supreme Court." *Los Angeles Times*, 22 December 2009. articles.latimes.com/2009/dec/22/nation/la-na-asian-carp22-2009dec22.

Lomolino, Mark, et al., eds. *Biogeography*. 4th ed. Sunderland, Mass.: Sinauer Associates, 2010.

Malanson, George. Personal interview, 9 September 2011.

McKibben, Bill. *Eaarth: Making a Life on a Tough New Planet*. New York: Times Books, 2010.

McPhee, John. *Annals of the Former World*. New York: Farrar, Straus and Giroux, 1998.

Menon, Shaily. "Asian Carp Frenzy: It's War! (Or So We're Told)." *Wake: Great Lakes Thoughts and Culture* 1, no. 2 (2012): 18–25.

Minteer, Ben A., and James P. Collins. "Move It or Lose It? The Ecological Ethics of Relocating Species under Climate Change." *Ecological Applications* 20, no. 7 (2010): 1801–4.

Parola, Philippe. "The Asian Carp Solution." Silverfin Marketing Group. cantbeatemeatem.us.

Ricciardi, Anthony, and Daniel Simberloff. "Assisted Colonization Is Not a Viable Conservation Strategy." *Trends in Ecology and Evolution* 24, no. 5 (2009): 248–53.

Rogner, John. Personal interview, 20 March 2012.

Sigma-Aldrich. "Material Safety Data Sheet: Rotenone R8875, Version 1.2." 29 June 2004. www.chemtrack.org/MSDSSG/Trf/msdse/msdse83-79-4.pdf.

Tip of the Mitt Watershed Council. "Asian Carp—Court Cases and Legal Action." www.watershedcouncil.org/court-cases-and-legal-action.html.

RECYCLE PRAIRIE DOGS

Andelt, W. F., and S. N. Hopper. "Managing Prairie Dogs." Colorado State University Extension, March 2016. extension.colostate.edu/topic-areas /natural-resources/managing-prairie-dogs-6-506.

Axtman, Kris. "The Prairie Dog: Pest or Pet?" *Christian Science Monitor*, 13 August 2002. www.csmonitor.com/2002/0813/p03s01-usgn.html.

Baron, David. *The Beast in the Garden: A Modern Parable of Man and Nature.* New York: Norton, 2004.

Crew, Bec. "Catch the Wave: Decoding the Prairie Dog's Contagious Jump-Yips." *Scientific American*, 7 January 2014. blogs.scientificamerican.com /running-ponies/catch-the-wave-decoding-the-prairie-doge28099s -contagious-jump-yips.

Food and Drug Administration. "Control of Communicable Diseases; Restrictions on African Rodents, Prairie Dogs, and Certain Other Animals." 8 September 2008. www.fda.gov/OHRMS/DOCKETS/98fr/FDA -2003-N-0427-nfr.pdf.

Graves, Russell A. *The Prairie Dog: Sentinel of the Plains.* Lubbock: Texas Tech University Press, 2001.

Hawkins, Chester Losey. Personal interview, 7 August 2015.

Leopold, Aldo. *A Sand County Almanac, and Sketches Here and There.* New York: Oxford University Press, 1949.

Moore, Evan. "Texas Prairie-Dog Catcher Enjoys Fame." *Houston Chronicle*, 1 December 2002. www.chron.com/news/houston-texas/article/Texas -prairie-dog-catcher-enjoys-fame-2099143.php.

National Geographic. "Prairie Dogs." www.nationalgeographic.com/animals /mammals/group/prairie-dogs.

National Park Service. "Blacktail Prairie Dog—Cynomys ludovicianus." 10 April 2015. www.nps.gov/wica/learn/nature/blacktail-prairie-dog -cynomys-ludovicianus.htm.

Watson, Lynda. Personal interview, 7 August 2015.

Williams, Ted. "The Prairie Dog Wars." *Mother Jones*, January 2000. www .motherjones.com/politics/2000/01/prairie-dog-wars.

World Health Organization. "Monkeypox." November 2016. www.who .int/mediacentre/factsheets/fs161/en.

EVOLVING THE MONSTER: A HISTORY OF GODZILLA

Blair, Gavin J. "'Godzilla Resurgence': Five Things to Know about Toho's Monster Reboot." *Hollywood Reporter*, 10 August 2016. www.holly woodreporter.com/heat-vision/godzilla-resurgence-five-things -know-918617.

Dello Stritto, Frank J. *A Quaint & Curious Volume of Forgotten Lore: The Mythology & History of Classic Horror Films*. Los Angeles: Cult Movies Press, 2003.

Dorkly Toplist. "Best Giant Monster." www.dorkly.com/toplist/62786/giant -monster.

Hongo, Jun, and Chieko Tsuneoka. "Godzilla Was Very Different 60 Years Ago." *Wall Street Journal*, 30 October 2014. www.wsj.com/articles /godzilla-was-a-very-different-beast-60-years-ago-1414666269.

Kalat, David. *A Critical History and Filmography of Toho's Godzilla Series*. Jefferson, N.C.: McFarland, 1997.

Lankes, Kevin. "Godzilla's Secret History." *Huffington Post*, 22 June 2014. www.huffingtonpost.com/kevin-lankes/godzillas-secret-history_b _5192284.html.

Pruitt, Sarah. "When Godzilla Attacked Tokyo." *History Channel*, 3 November 2014. www.history.com/news/the-original-godzilla-attacks-tokyo.

Quammen, David. *Monster of God: The Man-Eating Predator in the Jungles of History and the Mind*. New York: Norton, 2003.

Sasahara, Koji. "Japan's Latest Godzilla Movie Draws on 1954 Original, Fukushima Nuclear Disaster." *Columbus (Ohio) Dispatch*, 7 August 2016. www.dispatch.com/content/stories/life_and_entertainment/2016 /08/07/1-japans-latest-godzilla-movie-draws-on-1954-original -fukushima-nuclear-disaster.html.

Schilling, Mark. "'Shin Godzilla': The Metaphorical Monster Returns." *Japan Times*, 3 August 2016. www.japantimes.co.jp/culture/2016/08/03 /films/film-reviews/shin-godzilla-metaphorical-monster-returns/# .V6vnV5MrJE4.

Scott, A. O. "Still Radioactive and Spoiling for a Fight." *New York Times*, 15 May 2014. www.nytimes.com/2014/05/16/movies/godzilla-grandaddy -of-movie-monsters-stomps-back.html.

Tsutsui, William. *Godzilla on My Mind: Fifty Years of the King of Monsters*. New York: St. Martin's Griffin, 2004.

THE GREAT STORY OF THE STINKING CEDAR IN THE GARDEN OF EDEN

Acupuncture Today. "Torreya Seed (fei zi)." www.acupuncturetoday.com /herbcentral/torreya_seed.php.

Appell, David. "Can 'Assisted Migration' Save Species from Global Warming?" *Scientific American*, 3 March 2009. www.scientificamerican.com /article/assited-migration-global-warming.

Barlow, Connie. Personal interview, 20 September 2011.

———. "Rewilding *Torreya taxifolia*." Torreya Guardians website. www. torreyaguardians.org/rewilding.html.

Barlow, Connie, and Paul S. Martin. "Bring *Torreya taxifolia* North—Now." *Wild Earth*, Fall/Winter 2004–5, 52–56.

Callaway, Elvy E. *The Other Side of the South*. Chicago: Daniel Ryerson, 1934.

Hellmann, Jessica. Personal interview, 21 October 2011.

Hitchens, Christopher. "The Road to West Egg." *Vanity Fair*, May 2000. www.vanityfair.com/news/2000/05/hitchens200005.

Jahoda, Gloria. *The Other Florida*. New York: Scribner's, 1967.

Marinelli, Janet. "Guardian Angels." *Audubon*, May/June 2010. www .torreyaguardians.org/guardian-angels-audubon.pdf.

Marris, Emma. "Moving on Assisted Migration." *Nature*, 28 August 2008. www.nature.com/climate/2008/0809/full/climate.2008.86.html.

———. *Rambunctious Garden: Saving Nature in a Post-Wild World*. New York: Bloomsbury, 2011.

McLachlan, Jason. Personal interview, 21 October 2011.

Nijhuis, Michelle. "Taking Wildness in Hand: Rescuing Species." *Orion*, May/June 2008. orionmagazine.org/article/rescuing-species.

Ricciardi, Anthony, and Daniel Simberloff. "Assisted Colonization Is Not a Viable Conservation Strategy." *Trends in Ecology and Evolution* 24, no. 5 (2009): 248–53.

Robbins, Jim. *The Man Who Planted Trees: Lost Groves, the Future of Our Forests, and a Radical Plan to Save Our Planet*. New York: Spiegel and Grau, 2012.

Thomas, Chris D. "First Estimates of Extinction Risk from Climate Change." In *Saving a Million Species: Extinction Risk from Climate Change*, edited by Lee Hannah, 11–28. Washington, D.C.: Island Press, 2012.

———. "Translocation of Species, Climate Change, and the End of Trying to Recreate Past Ecological Communities." *Trends in Ecology and Evolution* 26, no. 5 (2011): 216–21.

Wilensky-Lanford, Brook. *Paradise Lust: Searching for the Garden of Eden*. New York: Grove Press, 2011.

Zimmer, Carl. "A Radical Step to Preserve Species: Assisted Migration." *New York Times*, 23 January 2007. www.nytimes.com/2007/01/23 /science/23migrate.html.

EPILOGUE: THE GENEALOGY OF EXTINCTION

Broswimmer, Franz. *Ecocide: A Short History of the Mass Extinction of Species*. London: Pluto Press, 2002.

Budiansky, Stephen. *Nature's Keepers: The New Science of Nature Management*. New York: Free Press, 1995.

Flannery, Tim. *The Weather Makers: How Man Is Changing the Climate and What It Means for Life on Earth*. New York: Grove, 2005

Hallam, Tony. *Catastrophes and Lesser Calamities: The Causes of Mass Extinctions*. Oxford: Oxford University Press, 2005.

Jablonski, David. "The Evolutionary Role of Mass Extinctions: Disaster, Recovery and Something In-between." In Taylor, *Extinctions*, 151–78.

Madrigal, Alexis C. "The Blood Harvest." *Atlantic*, 26 February 2014. www .theatlantic.com/technology/archive/2014/02/the-blood-harvest /284078.

McGhee, George R., Jr. *The Late Devonian Mass Extinction: The Frasnian/Framennian Crisis*. New York: Columbia University Press, 1996.

Morton, Timothy. *Ecology without Nature: Rethinking Environmental Aesthetics*. Cambridge, Mass.: Harvard University Press, 2007.

Prothero, Donald R. *Catastrophes!: Earthquakes, Tsunamis, Tornadoes, and Other Earth-Shattering Disasters*. Baltimore: Johns Hopkins University Press, 2011.

Raup, David M. *Extinction: Bad Genes or Bad Luck?* New York: Norton, 1991.

Shelley, Mary. *The Last Man*. 1826. Reprint, Oxford: Oxford University Press, 1998.

Taylor, Paul D. "Extinctions and the Fossil Record." In Taylor, *Extinctions*, 1–34.

———, ed. *Extinctions in the History of Life*. Cambridge: Cambridge University Press, 2004.

Temperton, James. "'Now I Am Become Death, the Destroyer of Worlds': The story of Oppenheimer's Infamous Quote." *Wired*, August 9, 2017, http://www.wired.co.uk/article/manhattan-project-robert -oppenheimer.

Ward, Peter D. *Under a Green Sky: Global Warming, the Mass Extinctions of the Past, and What They Can Tell Us about Our Future*. New York: Smithsonian Books, 2007.

Wignall, Paul B. "Causes of Mass Extinctions." In Taylor, *Extinctions*, 119–50.

Wing, Scott C. "Mass Extinctions in Plant Evolution." In Taylor, *Extinctions*, 61–98.